FHM
TRUE STORIES

THIS IS A CARLTON BOOK

Text copyright © Emap Elan Network 2002
Illustrations copyright © Nichant Choksi 2002
Design copyright © Carlton Books Limited 2002

This edition published by Carlton Books Limited 2002
20 Mortimer Street
London W1T 3JW

A CIP catalogue record for this book is available from the British Library.

ISBN 1 84222 703 3

Editorial Manager: Judith More
Art Director: Penny Stock
Executive Editor: Zia Mattocks
Editor: Sian Parkhouse
Typesetters: e-type
Production Manager: Sarah Corteel
Illustrator: Nishant Choksi (nish@nishantchoksi.com/www.nishantchoksi.com)

Thanks to FHM's readers for all their true stories

Typeset by E-Type, Liverpool
Printed and bound in Great Britain

www.fhm.com

FHM
TRUE STORIES

CARLTON
BOOKS

CONTENTS

Chapter 1 Work Antics   6

Chapter 2 Holiday High Jinks   40

Chapter 3 Sexual Shenanigans   61

Chapter 4 Animals & Children   81

Chapter 5 Injuries Endured   103

Chapter 6 Drunken Exploits   124

Chapter 7 Sober Humiliation   152

Chapter 8 Brushes With The Law   186

WORK ANTICS

DOG GOES AIRBORNE
Army ejects terrier

This happened when I was a young gunner working in Canada, a few years ago. I was operating a Challenger Battle Tank on a live firing exercise one afternoon when we were told by our commanding officer to expect a visit from a high powered general, and that best behaviour was required. After a few hours of live firing, the order came through to cease fire, and the tanks rumbled out of the greenery to form a neat line for the General's arrival. He arrived by helicopter and, with a small white Scottish terrier under his arm, swiftly made his way along the tanks introducing himself to everyone. When he reached our tank he clambered aboard for a quick look around, patted us all on the back, said, 'Right ho, chaps,' climbed off the machine and walked back to his helicopter to get an aerial view of the tanks firing their guns at predetermined targets. As we advanced into position I saw my first target and shouted up to the loader to arm the gun. As he stuck his hand in the charge bag however, he suddenly withdrew it with a loud 'Ouch,' and I turned to see the General's dog with its teeth clamped to the hand of the burly Irish gunner. Angry beyond belief, the gunner suddenly pushed the dog into the barrel of the 120mm gun, slammed the breach closed, looked at me and bellowed 'Fire!' In the heat of the moment I nodded grimly and pulled the trigger; the slobbering canine left our Challenger at mach three, and the spotters radioed through that the General was impressed by our accuracy.

ROYAL TAKES CHARGE
Oil worker offends inbred

In the Seventies I was working out in the North Sea on the Claymore Alpha Oil rig. One day we were notified of an impending visit from Prince Charles, and the guy in charge of the deck, a Canadian and staunch Royalist – ran us ragged for weeks, taking us through the landing drill over a dozen times. Once the helicopter had landed, the heli-crew would have to wait for the pilot to switch off a flashing red light under the fuselage before they could open the doors. The big day came and it was a scorcher – beautiful sunshine and not a breath of wind. The RAF Sea King appeared and made a perfect touchdown, but although the engines started to slow, the fuselage warning light kept flashing. We waited and waited and then, realising that his drill was starting to fall apart, the Canadian began gesturing to the pilot to turn the light off. He pointed under the aircraft and twirled his fingers frantically, but the confused pilot shrugged his shoulders and shook his head. Furious, the Canadian grabbed the radio and yelled into it, 'Turn off your fucking red light so we can approach your fucking aircraft, you goddam fucking idiot!' The pilot gave an immediate thumbs up and the light went out. He then slowly removed his sunglasses and pulled off his helmet: Prince Charles had opted to fly the helicopter himself that day.

BLIND MAN BETRAYED

Hospital humiliation for injured worker

I am a self-employed joiner who works away from home, and the following disaster happened to me last year when I was working at a hotel complex in London. I was using an angle-grinder and had a slight accident with a grinding disc. The disc shattered and left a really nasty gash just above my eye, an injury which needed 20 stitches. On the way to the hospital the ambulance medic bandaged both of my eyes shut and told me not to try to open them as this could result in more damage to my eye. After waiting on a hospital bed for over two hours I told my mate, who had come along to give me moral support, that I needed a pee, and he agreed to guide me to the loo. We walked aimlessly around the corridors for several minutes until I was really desperate. Finally, we walked through some doors and my friend positioned me in front of the bowl. I pulled out my cock and sighed, letting the hot gushing stream hit the pan. In seconds I heard howls of laughter and felt a hand on my arm. Then a woman's voice calmly asked me if I would mind not peeing in the wastepaper basket of the outpatient's department. My friend had calmly let me get my todger out in full view of over 20 other patients.

ORDERLY CONFUSES PASTE

OAP's foot & mouth mix-up

Many years ago I worked as a hospital orderly looking after elderly, senile patients. One particular woman didn't need much looking after, but understanding any of her requests was tricky due to her severe speech impediment, coupled with the fact that she wore cheap, ill-fitting dentures. One day, I decided to help her out by giving these stained gnashers a good clean, so I gently teased them from her chops and gave them a thorough scrub in the sink. I was proud to see that they looked absolutely gleaming when I had finished, and when I jammed them back in she had a true, gleaming, Hollywood smile. As I set about tidying the rest of the room, however, she suddenly started rolling around the bed and whimpering. There was also blood streaming out of her gob. Racing over, I grabbed her head, whipped out her dentures and dragged her over to the sink to wash her mouth out. It was only as the old dear was spitting down the drain that I saw the words 'Fungal Foot Cream' printed across what I had supposed to be the toothpaste tube.

PATIENT FORGETS AMPUTATIONS
Slippers elude searcher

Many years ago, I worked as an orderly in a local hospital. Although the sight of blood didn't bother me, I could never come to terms with the geriatric ward, where the old timers would continually cast aside blankets, offering me a display of their saggy breasts and greying, dilapidated pubic thatches. To make matters worse, one particularly senile woman mistook me for a wartime spiv, and demanded nylon stockings and bacon whenever I passed. Naturally I always ignored her, but one morning she changed her patter and asked me to fetch her slippers from under the bed. I got down on my knees and looked, but when I explained that they weren't there, she went berserk, shouting, 'What's wrong with you? Why can't you see them?', which was enough to convince me I simply wasn't looking hard enough. Just as it was getting to the stage where I was lifting the bed to look in the corners, the duty nurse tapped me on the shoulder and asked me what I was doing. When I explained I was hunting for the woman's slippers, she simply shook her head and through stifled laughter pointed at a gap in the bed – the precise gap where the old bat's legs should have been.

WORD MIX-UP
Policeman makes a big mistake

As a fresh-faced member of the Metropolitan Police Force, I was once asked to deal with a case of an old Jewish lady who had tragically attempted to take her own life. My partner at the time was an officer with numerous years of experience, and when we arrived at the hospital he propped himself up outside the nurses' rest area and informed me that I would be conducting the interviews. But while he stood there with his chest puffed out, the distraught daughter of the Jewish lady walked up and proceeded to embark on a long tale of suffering and pain, describing in great detail her mother's third suicide attempt. Evidently my partner's concentration had been entirely focused on the young girls in uniform, because he suddenly leant forward and, with as much sincerity as he could muster, boomed, 'Yes – it's tragic, isn't it? It almost makes you believe there's a real case for genocide.' We all stopped what we were doing and a stunned silence followed, before the daughter managed, 'You mean euthanasia, surely?' Realizing his blunder, my colleague nodded, then silently shuffled out of the room, to spend the rest of the afternoon sitting shamefaced in the patrol car.

ROAD SIGN NO USE
Squaddie loses way

This story dates back to when I worked at a parachute-training unit in Germany. We had a foreign skydiving team training with us, and at the end of their stay one of the lads was tasked with driving them to Hanover airport for their flight home. It was a three-hour round trip, and after six hours we started to worry. A quick call to the airport confirmed that he had dropped the team off, so we knew he was somewhere on the road back. Then the phone rang, and a rather panicky squaddie explained that he was lost and had run out of diesel for the van. To make matters worse, he only had one Deutschmark for the phone, and the pips were starting to go. Thinking quickly, we asked him if he could see any street signs to indicate his position. There was a brief pause, and then he excitedly replied 'I can see a sign for Rollsplitt. Oh thank God, I'm in Rollsplitt ...' before getting cut off. It sounded familiar, but none of us could place it, so we asked our German accountant. 'Rollsplitt?' he asked, completely deadpan, 'but that means loose chippings.'

ENGINEER INSPECTS FIREARM
Spud gun fun goes awry

Several years ago I worked night shifts as an electrical maintenance engineer. To pass the time, the team started to devise stupid ways of producing the loudest noise possible. The best technique was to place a mixture of oxygen and acetylene welding gas into a crisp packet, and light it at arm's length, but I developed the idea and came up with 'The Spud Cannon'. Basically a steel pipe with two gas taps and a spark plug, the cannon's power was breathtaking, and could easily put a King Edward clear over the horizon. All was well, until someone stuffed in a soggy tea bag, soaking the spark plug. I loaded and reloaded several times, but to no avail. It was then I made a critical error and ignored the rule, 'never look down the barrel of a gun'. Peering in to see if a spark was being produced, I pulled the trigger. There was a deafening noise, I went blind, and for a split second I thought I had blown my face off. When I got to a mirror, I realized I had singed my eyebrows and hair, huge pieces of rust from the pipe were embedded in my bleeding nose, and red welts showed where bits of tea leaf had peppered me.

ALCOHOLIC ACTS DECEASED
Helpful copper causes anguish

While on duty in the East Midlands, I was sent to an address following a report that the owner of the house had died. The tip had come from a well-known wino, who claimed that he had popped around to his mate's house and found him dead. Unable to stay in the house with the body, he said that he would wait outside the premises until I arrived. When I got there, a crowd of concerned locals, including the deceased's family were standing around, but the wino was nowhere to be seen. The door was firmly locked, but I could see that the upstairs window was ajar, and as everyone was becoming increasingly agitated, I called the fire brigade. Some time later, with a large audience, including six firemen, I ascended the ladder. When I got to the window I could see the body on the sofa, tongue hanging out, and lifeless. But as I opened the window and climbed in he sat bolt upright and looked straight at me. Excitedly I stuck my head out the window and shouted, 'He's alive.' Oh how the family members cried, and the firemen cheered, as they all waved happily at me. And then I felt a tap on the shoulder. 'I suppose you've come for the dead guy in the bedroom,' the wino said. Sheepishly I stuck my head back out and said, 'Actually, he *is* dead. Sorry.'

IN-FLIGHT TERROR
Pilots get locked out

While on a flight across China to take up a post with a minerals exploration company, I was too busy enjoying the spectacular view to bother too much about the slapdash standard of service. It wasn't until a stewardess entered the cockpit shouting at the top of her voice that I realized this was no ordinary flight. After a bit of a barney on the flight deck, she emerged, followed by the co-pilot, and they carried on their heated discussion in front of the passengers.

When they'd finished, the co-pilot turned to go back into his cabin, only to realize that the door had jammed. After much rattling, shaking and knocking, the captain came out to demand what was going on. He stepped out of the cockpit and closed the door behind him in order to deliver a stern lecture to his subordinates. It was only when they tried to open the door again that they realized it had jammed once more. This time, there was no-one left on the flight deck to open the door from the inside, and the captain, his co-pilot and the stewardess were getting more and more frantic as the door wouldn't budge. The passengers were also going mad, and it wasn't until someone found an emergency axe that they chopped down the door and regained the cockpit. For the rest of the flight, we could see the two embarrassed pilots through the splintered hole in their door, glaring at each other like mortal enemies.

OFFICER'S MESS
Swedes tempt frisky cop

While performing my duties as an Edinburgh police officer, my partner Colin and I had reason to stop a motorist, who was driving somewhat erratically. As I got out of the car to talk to him, two healthy young blondes started chatting to Colin, who was still sitting in the passenger seat. I spoke to the motorist, decided that he had been drinking, and asked him to accompany me back to the squad car. As he climbed into the back seat I couldn't help but notice that Colin had now exited the vehicle, was flirting like crazy with the giggling blondes, and was even showing them his handcuffs. I got in beside the worried motorist, prepared the breathalyser for the breath test, and put on the sternest face possible to read Section Six of the Road Traffic Act. However, no sooner had I uttered the words 'Now then, sir' when Colin dived into the front seat, slammed the door shut, turned to the pair of us and said: 'She's Swedish, and says if we give her and her a friend a lift up the road, she'll suck my cock!'

We stared at Colin's beaming face in stunned silence, until the police radio suddenly garbled a message. In a huge fit of laughter I told the motorist that we had an urgent call to attend and he was free to go. His bemused face, as he stood in the middle of the road and watched us roar off, will stick in my mind for ever.

FAST TRACKS
Squaddies take up race

While serving out in Africa many years ago as a regular in the army, a mate of mine, Joe, found himself sitting on the roof of an old Bedford bus, heading into the local town with the rest of his mates for what promised to be an almighty piss-up. As they hurtled down the dusty road, a great cheer suddenly went up from the front of the bus as it pulled out and began to slowly overtake a ramshackle pick-up truck. The little pick-up was being driven by an African family, and they were loving the attention, smiling and waving and doing their best to get a race going as the drunken squaddies slowly rumbled past. What was really making the boys laugh, however, was the grandmother. Due to the severe lack of space, she had been rolled up in a dirty red carpet and strapped to the roof rack. With only her wrinkled face visible, she jutted out about five foot in front of the truck, leading the charge with grim determination. Then, as Joe's bus inevitably pulled away, she emitted a banshee-like wail as she disappeared in a cloud of dust and diesel.

LOCAL POULTRY
Sailors regret chicken dinner

In 1995 I was in the Royal Navy serving onboard HMS Southampton in the West Indies. Visiting the islands in the Caribbean while doing our country's bit for the counter-drugs operation, one of our stops was the island of Montserrat. Our stay took the usual form of getting ashore and downing as much low-priced white rum as possible. Every bar seemed to offer much the same as the last: cheap booze and identical menus containing 'mountain chicken' and chips. After the fourth, we were starving and being adventurous we all opted for the chicken. When it came there only seemed to be chicken legs. The barman explained that because of the mountainous island, the legs of the mountain chicken were very big and the best part, so we tucked in. Two months later, when the island's volcano erupted, we were called back to aid in the disaster relief operation. We were erecting tents for the islanders to wait out the eruptions when, during a break, the biggest bullfrog we had ever seen – as big as a small dog – bounded across the field. We all laughed as this enormous amphibian hopped by. The laughter soon stopped when an old woman who was chasing it shouted, 'Hey, stop that mountain chicken!'

EARLY SHOUT
Fireman suffers slow burn

I'm a member of the fire service, and recently had to have a vasectomy. The night before the operation I received a phone call from a nurse Smithers, confirming my appointment and reminding me to bring a pair of tight underpants and fresh urine and sperm samples. The urine sample did not prove a problem, but the sperm donation reduced my wife to hysterics as I struggled nervously – the morning of the operation – to beat my non-responsive member into action. Finally my pathetic secretions were bottled, and off I went to hospital. The operation was a success, but I was slightly annoyed when the medical staff ignored my hard-won samples – although by the time my wife arrived to take me home I was past caring. It was only when I returned to work that I discovered that 'nurse Smithers' was in fact a work colleague, and that, during the 09:00hr parade – just about the time I was beating my floppy member into oblivion – a full squad of 22 firefighters had performed a mass groan of sympathy.

SUSPECT DEVICE
Soldier's heroics backfire

I am presently on a tour with a rifle company, serving in Belfast. While out and about a few months ago I noticed something which I thought required my expertise as a Unit Search Advisor: near a large tree a plank had been put across a hole in the ground, and leaves had been scattered over the board in an attempt at concealment. I went over with a member of my unit. We pulled the plank clear, and bingo! I found a small box, eight inches by four inches, the same size as a TPU (timer power unit) – a component in many of the terrorist devices used in the province. On closer inspection I saw that the box was made of cardboard, and I gingerly removed the lid. Inside, I saw a package wrapped in a handkerchief, with what looked like a piece of string sticking out of it. I decided to uncover the device, and at this point my company commander suggested we call in the experts. I resisted, seeking the glory for myself. I gently lifted the string and the handkerchief fell away. At that moment, my place in battalion legend became secure: the string was in fact a tail. In the torch beams we stared at a dead hamster, ruthlessly plucked from its lovingly constructed grave.

DETERRENT MISUSED
Bobby belts enraged beast

This story dates back to when I was a police probationer, being shown the ropes by an experienced copper called Baz. We were on routine patrol one night when a call was received of 'intruders on the premises' at a local breaker's yard. Baz was all too aware that the place was guarded by a vicious Rottweiler named Sid, so when we arrived he pulled out his trusty Halon fire extinguisher – an exceptional deterrent when sprayed into an animal's eyes. Our shift sergeant duly arrived and confidently led the way into the dark yard. No sooner had we rounded the first corner when the slavering Sid confronted us, baring his teeth and growling with intent. Then he charged us. Rather than run however, the sergeant decided he was Crocodile Dundee and attempted to out-stare the beast. It didn't work, and when Sid was a mere 15 metres away, Baz grabbed the extinguisher and yelled 'Here, sarge, use this!' The sarge nodded grimly, took it and swung it high over his head, bringing it down on the leaping mutt's cranium with a massive thud, killing it outright. 'Not quite what I had in mind, sarge,' was all a bemused Baz could say.

HAIR LOSS
Helpful worker causes pain

Some years ago, a mate of mine worked in the drawing office of a building company near Manchester. Every Friday they would go for a drink with the office girls, including a 40-year-old, size-18 receptionist, who habitually wore a white blouse which was virtually see-through. On this particular day they took their seats in the sun, and the receptionist sat opposite the newest draughtsman, who noticed that a hair had fallen down onto her shirt. Keen to appear friendly, he leaned over and gave a hearty tug, only to pull out possibly the world's longest, darkest nipple hair. It came out with such force that her whole boob lunged forward, and her scream brought the entire pub to a standstill. To top it all off, the surprised man dropped the hair in her pint, where it floated like a drowned worm, while all at the table tried to smother their guffaws of delight.

WELCOME TO BOSNIA
Copper's 'friendly' fire

My mate Norm is a copper who often had to work the night shift. To relieve the tedium, the bobbies devised a game: cowboys and Indians. They would stalk each other in the dead of night, while the town slept peacefully. Norm was a cowboy, but, being a bit slow, he was often subjected to vicious barrages of arrows. So, in order to exact revenge, he bought himself a blank-firing pistol. However, after two weeks of patrolling his territory, without seeing any Injuns, he began to wonder whether he was ever going to christen his peacemaker. One evening, having stopped in a doorway for a break, he could suddenly hear approaching footsteps. 'Ha!' thought Norm. 'This has got to be an Indian.' Out came the peacemaker and, with a devilish glint in his eye, Norm waited. Then, as the adrenalin pumped and the sweat dripped off his brow, Norm jumped into the street and shot at the Indian. But, to his horror, the victim was not an Indian. Norm vividly recalls watching his gun smoking, while an innocent member of the public lay sprawled on the floor, suffering a severe shock and involuntary urination and defecation.

BUCKET CONTAINS SURPRISE
Workers get unwelcome shower

Last summer I found myself refurbishing The King Solomon Hotel in Israel with another Brit in an attempt to earn enough cash for a ticket home. Our job was to rip the tables, mirrors and beds out of the rooms and throw them 14 floors down into the skips below. In one such room my fellow worker discovered a sealed 20-litre bucket of shit, which had been used by previous labourers as a toilet. Not knowing what to do with it, he hurled it over the edge, and we watched it plummet down to the ground. To our surprise, it remained intact. We forgot about it until four days later, when the whole team was led out to the courtyard to empty the skips. Two lads climbed up onto the piles and started throwing rubbish down to us – which was when, to my horror, I noticed a familiar-looking bucket soaring through the air. With no time to offer a warning, I bailed out of the way as the bucket hit with an explosion of spicy gases, spraying everyone with a heady cocktail of human faeces and urine. The result was a spontaneous vomiting session, as grown men puked until they could no longer stand.

ROAD KILLER
Soldier causes fireworks

One chilly winter's night, while serving with the army in Northern
Ireland, I was manning a vehicle checkpoint when a Ford Transit
screeched to a halt and an off-duty soldier jumped out. He was in a state
of extreme shock and, when he had finally calmed down, he explained
that he had been driving back from Lisburn when he'd seen what he
thought was a body lying in the middle of the road. Fearing a possible
terrorist ambush and unable to stop in time, he had put his foot down
and ran straight over it. I asked him where the body was, and was
shocked when he stammered that he thought it was stuck under the van.
My friend, Taff, looked at me in disbelief, and gingerly bent down to look
underneath the Transit.

'There's a guy under there …' he said as he got to his feet. 'Oh my
God! What have I done!?' cried the squaddie, falling to his knees and
bursting into tears. '… It's Guy Fawkes,' said Taff.

WHEELCHAIR DECEPTION
Guide embarrasses punter

About five years ago I worked as a backstage tour guide for a well-
known television station. Part of the tour included an explanation of
the intricate details of the blue screen – where anything coloured blue
fails to show up on camera. To do this properly, my group had to climb
a near-vertical ramp and take their places in fitted seats, from where they
could see themselves embarking on a magical journey via the screen in
front of them. On this particular occasion I had a middle-aged lady in a
wheelchair on my tour, who for obvious reasons could not get up into
a chair, so I placed her at the front so that she could still see herself
and enjoy the show. As the ride began, I explained that if anyone was
actually wearing an item of blue clothing, it would look as if it had
disappeared. Trying not to leave anybody out, I pointed at the lady at
the front and said, 'Ladies and gentlemen, if you look you will see that
this lady is obviously wearing blue trousers, as you cannot see her
legs.' To my utter horror, she slowly turned towards me and replied,
'Actually, I don't have any legs.'

LITTLE VOICE
Shaky start for loo pals

I work in an impersonal building with around 500 people. I was therefore rather surprised one bright morning when a fellow employee – nonetheless a complete stranger – said 'Hi' as we stood at the urinals. I found this an odd time to be greeting anybody, but not wishing to seem rude I turned and said, 'Oh, hello.' I was then rather taken aback when he stared as if I was insane before muttering, 'Hello.' It wasn't until I sat back at my desk that it all became crystal clear. My new-found buddy's first greeting had simply been a fart.

RESTAURANT URINATION DISASTER
Closing time cock-up

About ten years ago, while serving with the RAF, a few of my fellow airmen and I were on exercise near a village in North Wales. The end-of-exercise binge coincided with FA Cup final Saturday and a large contingent of RAF lads descended on the local hostelry. The landlord agreed to keep the pub open all day, only closing between 5 pm and 6 pm to clean up and replenish the shelves. As soon as he had closed the door on us at 5 pm I felt the desperate need to urinate. The village was deserted and without public conveniences. I found an alleyway, which had a brick wall on one side and a large shop window on the other, which seemed to be painted from the inside with black paint. I was blissfully engaged in the most satisfying pee I had ever had when I was accosted in mid-stream by a burly Welshman who, in mixed English and Welsh, accused me of exposing myself and peeing against the window of a restaurant. Apparently, although I couldn't see in, 30 or 40 people, including a local landowner with his daughter and prospective son-in-law, and a contingent of nuns from a nearby convent, could see out! The worst part of the whole affair was that after the local police were called and gave me a good telling off in front of the locals, I was assured that no further action would be taken. On my return to base, though, I found that a summons had been served on my CO. I paid a £20 fine and lost several years seniority in rank.

FIRE AID

Red-cap troubles pensioner

While working as a military policeman, I was called to a hospital one evening to help move patients caught in a fire. With my partner 'Fez' Parker, I started to shift about 18 elderly folk, some of whom were ranting and raving. Fez and I would grab a gibbering old lady each, wrap them in blankets and jam them into wheelchairs, before threading our way through the inferno to the car park. We were making good progress when suddenly my passenger, obviously panicking, tried to dive out of the chair, forcing me to grab her and put her back. No sooner had we restarted when she gave a grunt and lunged forward. I tried to pull her back but her strength was phenomenal, forcing me to shout, 'Fez, stop! This one's trying to escape. We've got a jumper!' Fez simply burst into laughter. 'You've got her blanket wrapped around the front wheels,' he explained. Needless to say, she never thanked me.

WORKMAN STUCK

Hound gets hots for gasman

While working some time ago as a gasman in Manchester, I received a call on my radio asking me to assist another workman in the area. When I arrived at the house, I found the carpet rolled back and the head of my friend sticking out through a lifted floorboard. When he saw me, he shouted that he needed some extra pipe and nodded his head in the direction of his van. Unfortunately, the subsequent motion of his long hair and beard attracted the attention of the customer's poodle, who embarked on a sexual assault of such ferocity on my friend's head that his unthinking reaction was to try to stand up, jamming himself between the floorboards. With one paw covering his eye and another stuffed in his mouth, his furious head-shaking only served to excite the eager pooch to ever more energetic arousal: it was jerking away at breakneck speed, eyes crossed and tongue flapping wildly. Fortunately, just as it looked as if the dog was about to come in my mate's ear, the poodle's owner came flying in and booted the dog across the room. These days, my mate sports a crew-cut.

TROPHY WIVES
Car lads hoard pants

About a year ago, I sold used cars for a city-centre dealer. We worked out of two huge Portakabins, one nice and clean for the customers, the other a 'snake pit' for eight salesmen. It was horrific, full of dirty magazines, men swearing and filthy mugs. Our favourite item, however, was what we called the Trophy Tree. Basically, whenever we delivered a car, we would ask to use the toilet. While in there, a quick root through the laundry basket was undertaken, and the dirtiest pair of knickers stolen. The offending item then went on the tree, points being awarded on a scale of sauciness, amount of material soiled and sex-appeal of the owner. One day one of the lads was lounging around in our private cabin when the door flew open and in walked a customer. 'What's that?' laughed the bloke at the door, pointing at our tree. 'It's a trophy tree,' my friend Mark answered sheepishly, explaining that the boys brought in knickers from the girls they had scored with over the weekend. The customer thought it was brilliant and recounted bawdy tales of his youth. As he left he pointed at a nasty grey pair and sighed, 'That's all my missus wears these days, though.' We never heard from him again, but the awful fact is that they were the dirty grots of his beloved wife. Mark had stolen them the previous week.

TRAGIC HAIR LOSS
Last wish leads to job loss

Many years ago, while working as a care assistant at a nursing home, I had the pleasure of dealing with some lovely old people, several of whom, naturally, died while I was working there. We had one resident, Fred, who had a fine toupee, and it was his wish that when he died I made sure he was wearing his rug when he was laid to rest. Sadly, he did indeed die, and I was left with the task of preparing his body for the undertaker, and for his family to view. As I was preparing the old man I popped his toupee onto my head for 'safe keeping', and continued cleaning the body. Just as I was finishing, the phone in the corridor rang, and I ran out to answer it. While I was on the phone who should walk in but Fred's son, who instantly recognized his father's syrup on my head. So while Fred got his last request, I got the sack.

FHM WORK ANTICS

JUNGLE BOOGIE
Squaddie vs reptile

During a break from patrolling the jungle in Belize, my platoon stopped to enjoy a quiet afternoon of drinking and sunbathing. Spotting a turtle in a storm drain, we brought it over for a closer look. Its immediate response was to extend its neck slightly and open its beak in a gesture designed to frighten away pissed-up squaddies. While most of us could recognize an angry snapper turtle when we saw one, one guy – Tam – was blissfully ignorant, and we cringed as he held the livid creature at waist level, took his member out and laughingly demanded oral sex. Suddenly there was a blur of movement – the snapper had stretched out and clamped down on the idiot's meat and potatoes. We were then treated to the sight of a screaming Tam, charging through the jungle with an angry green turtle dangling from his cock. Amazingly, both parties survived, but we never did manage to ascertain who emerged most traumatized.

PLUMBING GAFF
Old boiler gets a shock

While relaxing after an enormous roast dinner one Sunday afternoon, the telephone rang. I am a plumber, so it is not unusual for me to get emergency call-outs, and sure enough, it was one of my elderly and more snooty customers. Apparently, her boiler was making unusual noises and she was worried it might explode. So, with much regret at having had my day off interrupted, I agreed to go over to her house. She met me at the front door and I asked her where the boiler was located. She informed me it was a wall-mounted boiler in the kitchen, over the worktop, so I walked through to the kitchen, thinking the old lady had stayed in the hall. In the kitchen, I climbed onto the worktop to inspect the boiler, but as I did so, I let out a fart of epic proportions. I was mortified, therefore, to find the lady of the house standing behind me with a look of contempt on her face. Thinking it would be too rude and obvious to simply apologize, all I could say was, 'Is the boiler making a noise similar to that?'

FINANCIAL FARRAGO
Sleepy bank wakes up

A few years ago, I was working in Southampton for a national bank as a trainee manager. Every couple of months or so, my boss would poke his head out of his office and despatch one of his boys off to some remote branch for 'a taste of the real world'. That's how, one rainy October morning, I found myself standing on a deserted railway platform far away in the Cheshire countryside. After wandering through the peaceful hamlet, I located the branch of my bank, where I was royally greeted and shown into a huge room – the regular manager was on holiday, and I could use his office. The assistant manager saw me settled in, then shut the door, screening off from my sight the bumpkins queuing up to cash their EC subsidies. I unpacked my briefcase, shuffled a few papers, and realized I didn't have a clue what to do next. Glancing around, I found a nice big button under an old copy of the *FT*. 'Tea!' I thought, and buzzed the assistant. I couldn't hear a thing, so I gave the buzzer another good old push. But my daydreaming was interrupted by a banshee wail. Rushing out, I was greeted by the sight of a middle-aged lady teller collapsed in tears in the street. I'd been pressing the silent alarm, and the poor woman

I'd terrified had just been transferred to the bucolic village. She had been held up at the Wolverhampton branch two weeks earlier.

FIREMAN FRAMED
Armed robber innocent

It was my third day as a fireman. My station was in two parts – one for the appliances, the other for tools and admin. My boss asked me if I could take some gear to be serviced at the second part of the station. I was wearing full kit – boots, orange trousers and black donkey jacket and they loaded me up with breathing apparatus (helmet on, as my hands were full). One of the guys handed me an old pickaxe handle which needed reheading. As I walked out of the station our office clerk handed me a deposit envelope, asking me to drop it into the bank on the way past. At the bank I attracted a few odd looks as I waited in the queue. Eventually I gave a cashier the envelope. She asked me to wait for my receipt. I leaned on the counter, leafed through a brochure and waited. And waited. Thinking she was taking her time, I looked up and she'd gone. Well, not exactly gone, but standing with the rest of the staff in a far corner looking past me at the bank's entrance. I followed her gaze and nearly shit myself. An armed policeman in a crouched firing position told me very firmly to drop the axe handle. As I did so another one grabbed me and handcuffed me. Only when we reached the station did they let me see the bank deposit envelope. On it was written: 'Give me all your money or I'll smash in the screen!'

BIRDS BLUNDER
Jets cause ostrich havoc

I work as an air traffic controller for the RAF, and we occasionally get people ringing up to complain about low-flying jets 'going under my washing line' or 'in between my hedges'. One night at work the switch-board lit up with people complaining about nine Tornadoes flying incredibly low. One call in particular has kept the entire fast jet community in stitches for months. A local farmer who kept ostriches called to say the jets were playing havoc with his birds. It's a well-known fact that ostriches stick their heads in the sand at the first sign of danger and it seems that they'd been so scared by the jets they'd instinctively tried to bury their bonces.

Sadly, the farmer had the flock standing on concrete at the time, and five of his beauties had rendered themselves unconscious trying to hide.

RUDE CORPSE
Dead man's final insult

While on a peacekeeping mission in Kosovo, I found myself leading an army patrol in the capital, Pristina. As soon as we arrived, my team of three was called to a block of flats where an Albanian had shot his Serb neighbour. On arrival we found that the victim lived on the 12th floor and weighed at least 20 stone, which posed the real problem of getting the bull-sized corpse outside. I got on the radio and asked if we could throw the whale out of the window, and received a prompt ear bashing, so we lugged him out to the knackered lift. Unfortunately, after dragging him in, neither of us could reach the buttons, and it was then that I was struck by true genius. The body was in the later stages of rigor mortis and, with Herculean strength, I managed to snap his middle finger up into a 'pointy' position and got him to press the ground floor button. He was taken to hospital 'flicking the bird,' and months later a medical friend told me of a mysterious case that his team had to deal with. They dubbed it 'The phenomenon of the pointy finger.'

ART APPRECIATION
Driver makes easy mistake

Some years ago, I worked as a bus driver for a local company. One beautiful summer's afternoon a very attractive young lady boarded my bus and, as she rummaged in her purse, a magnificent rose tattoo – located just at the top of her cleavage – was revealed to me in all its splendour.

As I took her fare, I thought that I would try my luck and make a compliment about her great body art. Looking her straight in the eye I gave my most engaging smile, leaned up to the glass and shouted, 'I like your tits!'

All explanations that what I had meant to say was 'tattoo' fell on deaf and somewhat angry ears as I was loudly harangued as a 'pervert' and 'dirty sod' in earshot of every other passenger on the bus.

SERVICE SUSPENDED
Worker offends congregation

One Sunday morning about ten years ago, I went with my road-gang to resurface a road in Seaford. We turned up early, hoping to beat the traffic, but were somewhat dismayed to find a large number of cars parked exactly where we needed to work. There was a large church nearby, and as I was the new boy, I was sent along to see if any of the worshippers owned any of the vehicles. Inside, the vicar was right in the middle of his sermon, so I stood at the back to try to catch his eye. Just as everyone knelt down to pray, my two-way radio burst into life: 'Holy shit! What the hell are all those cars doing here?' hollered one hairy-arsed pal. 'I bet it's those bastards in the church!' came the grumpy reply. As one, the angry congregation spun round to see a red-faced lad staggering out of church, fumbling with a radio. Needless to say we waited for the service to end before we started resurfacing the road.

DUMB DRIVER
Good Samaritan panics

Last year, I was driving to work in the morning when I noticed a man spread out face-down on the pavement. I slowed right down and watched him for a few seconds, and he appeared to be completely still. Worried, I parked the car and watched for a minute or so, but he remained absolutely motionless. I decided he must have either been knocked over or collapsed from a heart-attack, so I jumped out of the car and ran across to the pavement, screaming and shouting for help. When I got to the bloke, I grabbed him under the arms and tried to turn him over, just as a small crowd began to assemble around me. It only took me a few seconds to realize that he was, in fact, a workman with his arm down a manhole. He wanted to give me a panning for 'tickling' him while he was trying to work, but I eventually convinced him I was simply trying to be a good Samaritan and save his life.

RURAL RAGE
Farmer ruins sad day

I'm a farmer in a quiet, scenic part of south Yorkshire. There are rolling fields surrounded by lakes and woods — it really is a beautiful part of the world. However, as the school summer holidays coincide with harvest-time, we do have a problem with kids. They seem to delight in setting fire to 6ft-round bates of straw and rolling them downhill, so when I spotted a group of people gathered in a field I had baled earlier I was pretty angry and tore towards them on my tractor. The sight of a ten-tonne machine hurtling across a field must be pretty frightening, and it's usually enough to send the little terrors scarpering off. But as I got nearer they refused to budge. I blared my horn and shouted at them to get the hell out of my field. By the time I was right upon them I was furious. It was only then that I realized they were all in their forties and fifties and all wearing suits. Then an elderly lady said: 'I'm sorry, we're observing a minute's silence. We've just scattered my husband's ashes here as he loved this place so much.'

HOLE PUNCHER
Greek men feel inadequate

In 1974 I was serving in Cyprus with the RAF. I was sent for a week's firing practice near Famagusta. On our first evening, a long convoy of trucks, laden with Greek builders, drove up the hill past our camp. As they went by us, the tailgates dropped and, jeering, they all started urinating on the road, pointing at their members to imply that they were hung like donkeys. This happened each day, and by the third day we had seen enough. I found a long piece of hose that had been bleached white in the sun. As their ritual began I walked towards them, causing almost deafening levels of insults, and a mass display of swarthy penises. Then I pulled out the pipe and, with my own willy tucked inside it, began to pee onto the road while swinging it from side to side. The visual effect was stunning, my RAF chums went ballistic and three Greeks fell off the back of the truck. We never saw a single open tailgate again.

KITCHEN COCK-UP
Diner gets unsavoury sarnie

While working as a kitchen assistant in a bistro in Australia I formed a mischievous friendship with the chef. He and I were working one New Year's Day, when the bistro took record business. In the midst of a particularly panicky period, I was trying to set up an 'avocado cheese melt' open sandwich. I laid out two slices of bread and sliced the avocado at blur speed. But in my haste, I cut myself from thumb to wrist, splattering blood all over the meal. In shock, I ran off to put a plaster on. When I came back, the sandwich had disappeared, so I just got on with the next order. Later on, when we finally had a quiet spell, I commented how quickly the chef had finished making up the meal. He confessed: he'd just turned the avocado over and melted the cheese on top. Hey presto! Avocado cheese melt. Morbid laughter filled the kitchen area. We went to the dining area and identified the unsuspecting 'vampire', a beautiful blonde lady. Strange morbid laughter once more. A waitress came to inquire what the joke was. We recounted the tale, still hysterical. She replied, rather sternly, 'That's my best friend.' Ouch. Incidentally, the unsuspecting vampire left a big tip.

SAUSAGE SURPRISE
Soldiers enjoy hot meal

After ten years, I feel ready to make this confession. While serving in the Gulf back in 1991, I found myself alone in the back of my wagon on night-watch duties, while my two crewmates slept under the stars. It was about 5.30 in the morning and I was thinking about my fiancée when I struck upon an idea. Warming up a tin of sausages in the kettle, I removed the middle three, popped the can over my knob and proceeded to give my little fella a good thrashing. When I had finally finished, it was 6 am, and time for breakfast. I dutifully cooked up a culinary delight of beans, bacon burgers, eggs and, obviously, the spunky sausages. My crewmates wolfed the whole lot down and thanked me for the wonderful morning meal. I've not seen Keano or Skell for nine years, and if they are reading this, I hope I never see them again.

BREAK ERRAND
Youth makes stupid purchase

A few years ago, my father came home from work killing himself with laughter. Apparently a young guy had been taken on as part of a Youth Training Scheme to run the daily errands for the workers. On that particular day he had been given a list of requisites from the workmen, including Dave's, which was, 'Get me 20 Benson & Hedges, and if they don't have those, get me anything else.' When the teen returned he shared out all the goods, approached Dave, and said 'Sorry sir, there weren't any Benson And Hedges, so I got you this instead,' and handed him a Walls pork pie.

TOILET JOKE BACKFIRES
Barber embarrasses client

While waiting one day for a client to arrive at the hairdressing salon I manage, myself and one of the girls I worked with were sitting in the staff room, having a conversation about toilet habits. Soon, she went to the toilet and I decided to make coffee. On the way to the kitchen, I passed the toilets, and could not resist making rude noises and shouting, 'I know what you're doing!' Snickering, I walked into the kitchen and, to my horror, there was my colleague making coffee. I screamed, 'I thought you were going to the toilet!' She replied, 'Oh, I was, but your client arrived early and she's in there!' The next hour was the worst of my life.

UNPLEASANT JAPERY
Crunchy feast for prankster

I used to be the director of a company which built up a relationship with another firm sharing the building. To brighten our days, we would play practical jokes on each other. You know the sort of stuff: weird phone calls, condoms, hidden pornography. But we were being humiliated, so, having identified their best prankster, Bob, we took revenge. He had gone out, leaving his lunch-box helplessly vulnerable to attack. We cut our toenails, spread them into Bob's sarnies and waited for lunch. Not a single word. But we could all sense a case of Humour Systems Failure. As we were splitting our sides, he marched into our office and crammed his lunch into the fax machine, toenails and all, then stormed back out, calling us a bunch of sick bastards and slamming the door. Bob, rumour has it, now owns a restaurant. I think I'll give it a miss. Just in case.

DREADFUL CAREER MOVE
The man who dug trenches

When I was a student I was employed by a building firm during a summer holiday. Day one, start 7.30 am. I was given a pick and shovel and instructed to dig a trench 40 yards long, by two feet wide and three feet deep. This took three days. On the fourth day a surveyor came along and told the foreman that the trench was in the wrong place. I was then told to fill it in and re-dig it ten yards to the left. Four days later, tired, blistered and pissed off, I completed trench two only for another surveyor to come by and say that the first trench was correct after all and that I should fill the second trench in and re-dig the first one. I was not amused to say the least. Four days later both surveyors arrived and concluded that we didn't need any trenches and that I could just fill it in. And if they needed any more trenches dug they promised not to ask me. To this day I have a great aversion to holes.

TOILET BLOCKED
Workman stems flow

While working as a plumber I was called to a nasty blockage in the ladies toilet of a large office block. I lifted the inspection hatch, and attempted to remove the blockage with my arsenal of pipe cleaners. After 20 futile minutes, I decided there was nothing else for it, and shoved my arm up the main pipe to remove a dam built from shit and tissue. I was almost done when a woman entered the next cubicle. In an attempt not to scare her I lay still, while she laid the smelliest log known to man. When the toilet flushed I realized I was about to get whacked in the face by the giant curler, so I pushed my arm in far enough to completely block the pipe. As her panties disappeared from view, large warm lumps of poo clung to my arm like leeches. She never guessed I was there, but I smelt ripe for the rest of the day.

TANK REPULSION
Soldiers drink dirty water

While on exercise in Canada recently the temperature inside our armoured tank used to regularly creep above 100°F. As a consequence of this myself and my crew's intake of water was very high, even though it was usually warm enough to brew up with. During one part of the exercise while filling the internal drinking container from a jerry-can, I noticed a bad smell, which I put down to the heat of the plastic container. At dawn the following day, at the end of a particularly hot exercise, where we had to drink copious amounts of water, I decided we should all wash and clean up. I went first and very refreshing it was to wash and brush my teeth after a hard night of manoeuvres. It was then Ian, my gunner's, turn. He appeared to be having difficulty getting the remaining water from the jerry-can into the washing-up bowl. Then, with a very distinctive plop a pasty, white, hairless and obviously somewhat decayed corpse of a large rat dropped out. After a bout of dry heaving and the appropriate medical checks we then all had to endure weeks of witless Roland Rat jokes for the rest of our posting.

SALESMAN SCAMMED
Oldsters terrified by desperate man

Three years ago I was constructing a house for an old couple, who lived next door. One day we were laying bricks when a sales rep called Clive arrived, asking us where the toilet was. Quick as a flash, one of the lads explained that we all used the toilet next door, and Clive immediately scuttled off towards the house. To make matters worse, the labourer told him to put the kettle on, 'And don't worry about the old lady, she's just a cleaner.'
He was gone half an hour, and when he came out he was not a happy bunny. Apparently he had put the kettle on and then wandered down the hall to find the toilet. When the old dear came out, he said, 'Hello love, I'm just going to use the loo,' and the husband appeared and shouted, 'What the bloody hell is going on?' It was at that point Clive realized he had been stitched up, but he opted to blag it, and explained that he was a surveyor, checking for woodworm. Then he shut the toilet door and had a poo. When he emerged, the old man was standing there with a ladder and torch. 'Shall we start upstairs?' he asked, and Clive spent the next half an hour lifting up carpets checking for rotting wood.

RANDY FAUNA
Reindeer destroys show

After graduating from college, I spent the summer working in the souvenir shop at my local zoo. At the end of October however I still didn't have a full time job lined up. With the dole queue looking inevitable, I was then fortunately approached by the marketing manager who offered me a job until January – working in Santa's grotto. In an attempt to bolster sales figures they had hit upon the idea of including a live reindeer, and being of a jovial and jolly disposition, I was told I would play the bearded gent. Before the grotto opened we had a press call, and I was chauffeur driven up to the zoo to pose for the local journalists. Despite the enthusiastic reception from the crowd however, Prince the Reindeer was a very reluctant partner and refused to sprint alongside me for the action shots. Every time I began to run, Prince would pull in the opposite direction and knock me off my feet with a quick jerk of his head. The press persuaded me to have one

last attempt, and as I pulled his reins, the mighty beast began to follow. As I turned my back to him and shouted 'Ho, ho, ho,' I suddenly felt a hoof on each shoulder. In full view of the cameras and excited children, Prince then tried to shag me. I lost my Santa beard, hat and dignity as I wrestled with the randy mass of antlers, completely unaided by his keeper who was helplessly paralysed with laughter.

EMBARRASSING THESPIAN ERROR
The actor who forgot his lines

My friend was playing the character Christopher Wren in *The Mousetrap*. One Friday night performance the curtain went up and the play started its seemingly perpetual motion of some 34 years. After several unremarkable entrances and bits of routine dialogue – he'd been doing eight shows a week for six months – he came to his favourite scene, the part where he got to sit down on the settee and listen to the rest of the cast discuss the murderous events of the day. Musing on his strenuous partying that week while waiting for his cue he was overcome with a sense of panic at no longer recognizing the lines. Hearing someone going: 'Pssst, pssst', he looked up to the wings where he could see the Stage Manager waving him over. Uncertain whether to move for fear of missing his cue he hung on, only for the dialogue to become even more perplexing. Eventually the Stage Manager's emphatic beckoning and the small crowd of backstage staff gathered round her also signalling time-out convinced him it was time to leave the stage. When she finally hooked him into the wings she told him he'd been asleep for five minutes with the show going on around him, and to compound the felony he should have been in another part of the house providing other cast members with an alibi.

IMPROMPTU KARAOKE
Solitude shattered

Two years ago, desperately short of cash, I grudgingly took a job manning the till at a petrol station. Being the new boy, I was immediately assigned the graveyard shift: 11 pm to 1 am, and apart from the occasional car thief and insomniac the only real company I had was my Walkman. So imagine my delight when half-way through a particularly slow, soul-destroying shift I spotted my first customer in hours, steaming past the pumps towards my booth, perhaps for an urgent pint of semi-skimmed or packet of condoms. However, as the guy got nearer it became obvious that he was not a happy bunny. It turned out that he hadn't appreciated the last 45 minutes of my out-of-tune singalong to Semisonic over the forecourt tannoy, which I'd stupidly left switched on. Neither, it became apparent, were the rest of the nearby estate, nor my new boss, who after receiving umpteen complaints from weary locals gave me the boot.

NEW YEAR SURPRISE
Officer sifts poo

I am a prison officer and once worked in a segregation unit where any con who breaks prison rules normally ends up. My worst job involved searching human turds. Any inmate who is seen swallowing suspected drugs on a visit is kept in the segregation unit for a process charmingly called 'no slop out'. This means that the con is left in a cell with an adult-sized potty waiting for nature to take its course and the swallowed wrap of drugs to pass through. You would think that in our technically-advanced age there would be a device to search the contents of the pot. There is. It consists of a pair of rubber gloves and a catering-size sieve! It's not the job to do with a hangover. Last New Year's Day, after a night celebrating, it got the better of me and I threw up. I had to search the turds with diced carrot and tomato topping, but it cured the hangover, though.

ARMY HIGH JINX
Dumped right in it

While serving in Tidworth, I heard I was being posted at short notice. As a joke, the bloke across the corridor stole my cold-weather gear and pissed all over the contents of my bergen. I only discovered this when 3,500 miles away, freezing my bollocks off and stinking of piss. Back in Blighty, I went straight out on the piss then returned to the barracks, and noticed that my practical joker pal had left his window open. I climbed in and got busy writing 'WANKER!' in toothpaste on his duvet and pissing in his coffee mug, then throwing the contents onto his posters and family photos. Finally I curled the best aprés-vindaloo turd you ever saw under his bed. The next morning, I was halfway through shaving when the washroom door burst open and a 6ft 7in, 18-stone former Hampshire Schoolboys' lock-forward burst in and barked, 'Who's the fuckin' dead man who's shit under my bed and thrown piss at my parents?' I could barely hold my razor still. My previous neighbour had been posted to a new regiment while I was away. Please don't reveal my name – big, bad Gaz is still on the look-out.

STRANGE RELIGIOUS VISION
Driver leaves moving car

A few years ago I worked in an estate agent's office on the corner of a busy high road at the top of a gentle hill. We all parked our company cars on the side street. One Monday morning my car was parked close to the junction, in full view of the office. Someone noticed an old green Fiesta trundling around the corner, with three elderly ladies as passengers, no driver, the driver's door open and another elderly lady running behind the car shouting, dressed in black. She caught up with it just as it crashed into the back of my parked company car. My colleagues and I rushed out with me screaming for an explanation. The elderly lady turned on me, shocked at my bad language, and I saw that the black outfit was actually that of a nun. Her passenger, the Mother Superior, explained that Sister Mary had offered to nip into Boots on the opposite corner, but had forgotten she was driving and just stepped out of the slightly moving car, quickly realizing her mistake. With a wry smile my boss said to the Mother Superior: 'You realize the insurance will never pay up?' 'Why?' asked the horrified nun. 'Act of God,' he mused. The insurance did pay.

SCHOOL DAYS
Suspended plumber sees too much

I left school last year and started serving my apprenticeship as a plumber. One day the boss and I were called out on a job at my old school to mend a leak in the shower block roof. We dragged ourselves along the roof space to the hole, and once there, the boss decided that I could take care of things by myself. He said he could put up a 'No Entry' sign at the entrance, and then left. I pulled away a ceiling slab for better access and leaned right out to get beneath the hole. It was only when my old teacher – an ageing beast of 47 – wandered in below me that I realized the boss had forgotten the sign. I remained hanging there like a large spider inches above his head, as he spent ten minutes scratching his tiny cock, and guffing.

CANDID CAMERA
Gaseous escape captured

When I worked for a defence company, I was involved in a missile test. This sounds exciting, but in reality it meant spending a couple of weeks sitting in a concrete bunker waiting for the day to end, and the evening drinking to start. Early one morning, after a particularly heavy night on the ale, I was stuck as normal in my concrete prison – with no chance to get rid of the foul gas my digestive system was producing from the night before. So when someone asked me to go outside to adjust some equipment, I jumped at the chance, and within minutes had let rip with a by now considerable beer fart. After a few minutes spent freezing my arse off, I returned to the bunker, to find everyone gathered around a monitor, killing themselves laughing. I wandered over to take a look and watched as the clearly discernible infrared image of a person came into view, stopped, and bent over. The thermal display from my fart was actually quite impressive, and some clever sod even made it into a screensaver as my leaving present.

SPILLAGE ERROR
Punter drinks wrong lager

Shortly after acquiring a job in a particularly dingy night club, a punter at the bar asked me to mind his beer while he went to the toilet.

By the time the bloke returned for his half consumed beverage, I had completely forgotten my lager-minding responsibilities. In haste, I grabbed an unfinished but discarded pint from an uninhabited area of the bar and passed it to the punter. It was a bit warm, but he seemed pleased and said, 'Cheers mate, thought you'd lost it there.' He downed it in one, smiled and wandered off. Come the end of the night, I set about clearing the bar area. My colleague pointed to the end of the bar where I'd found the 'spare' pint and said, 'Don't clear that part of the bar. I always leave it to the cleaner.' He explained, 'It's right under the Gents and they leak. I normally put out a glass to collect the drips, but it's disappeared tonight.'

CAREER STALLED
The chicken man

When I left school in Devon at 16, I began the worst six weeks of my working life. Clocking in at 7 am in regulation Wellingtons, hair-net and white overalls, the day started with wedging bagged giblets up still-warm chickens' arses as they sped by on a conveyor belt. After a 15-minute break for breakfast, when all I could stomach was hot chocolate, it was into the freezer to sort the oven-readies into weight categories and a game of 'chicken footie'. After a quick dusting, the 'football' was put back on the conveyor, destined for a supermarket shelf. Watching the other workers at lunch gorging on platefuls of food (sometimes chicken) was almost enough to make me retch. But the biggest treat of the day came in the afternoon when the stench of the coagulated blood and excrement from around 30,000 chickens wafted around the factory floor with the flushing of the drains. I haven't eaten chicken for nine years.

CHOMPERS HIDDEN
Pensioner loses teeth

One of the few highlights of working on an acute medical ward centred around a sweet old dear who was admitted with severe dementia. It quickly became apparent that she was constipated and would need suppositories to get things going, which she claimed she could do herself. Later that morning, while she was getting washed, an enquiry was made on the whereabouts of her false teeth, to which she replied that she had stuck them up her arse. Finding the suppositories floating in her cornflakes, we decided that she could be right, and whisked her off to X-ray. Sadly, nothing was found. A week later she was still bunged up, so I gave her a mild enema and told her I'd be back in a few minutes. When I returned I was greeted by the sight of granny bending over the bed, with her winking starfish aimed squarely at my face. Then, as I rushed to help her, her arse slowly changed shape, and three front teeth briefly surfaced before being sucked back in. I stood there as her bottom grinned, then frowned at me, until the top set of chompers finally came flying out, followed by a wave of shit. To this day, the bottom set are still missing.

HOT NOSH
Builder hampered by diner

When I worked on a building site in Brighton, there was a lad there called Beanie. He was a fat, very rude chap, who had absolutely no qualms about wolf-whistling at women, while showing them his bare arse.

One morning in the local café, Beanie had just finished his breakfast when another builder sat down next to him, blocking him in. Beanie asked him to move, but the bloke refused, saying that he was starving and Beanie would just have to wait until he had finished. Not prepared to put up with this, Beanie stood on his stool and proceeded to try and step over the bloke's lap. As he did so, his shorts split open and his bollocks dropped straight out, dragging right through the bloke's mashed potato, leaving a great long spud trench, and a pair of painfully blistered balls.

FOREIGN LANGUAGE MIX-UP
Italian boss misunderstands

It was a Friday afternoon and I had just found out that the department I was expecting to head (I had recruited the staff, obtained the equipment, etc.) had been handed to someone else. Effectively this meant I would be made redundant. So I went to complain to my boss, an Italian. I was about to confront him when two visitors entered. Diplomatically, I told him it could wait until Monday and left. He followed me and demanded to know what was wrong. I bellowed at him 'I'll tell you what's wrong Giuseppe – I'm fucking ANGRY!' He stood silent for a second, looking puzzled before replying 'I 'ave some biscuits in my office if you are 'angry.' I didn't know whether to throw him off the balcony or jump myself.

PRINCESS NIGHTMARE
Royal nearly gassed on plane

While working as a crew member for an airline, we had to do a short hop from the Bahamas to Trinidad and back. After the passengers had boarded, news soon filtered down to 'chaos class' that Princess Anne and her entourage would be getting on, and that first class was a no-go area for us plebs working in economy. Unfortunately, I had unwisely tried a few of the local 'delicacies' and was subsequently suffering from a bad case of the trots, and the accompanying symptom known locally as 'Caribbean Ring'. Soon after take-off, my bowels decided to evacuate. I couldn't find a free toilet anywhere in the non-cordoned-off area of the plane, so I trespassed into a first class loo, where I unloaded the foulest toxic waste ever known outside Chernobyl. With my business done, I opened the door only to find myself face to face with HRH. After nervously bowing, I sped away, pausing only to glance back and watched her enter that gas chamber. At the very least, I hope I left the seat warm.

DECORATING DISASTER
Painter flees embarrassment

When I was struggling to earn a crust, and willing to take any work for any price, I once landed a job painting a friend of a friend's parents' house. I went round there on my first day and talked over the colours and details with the owners, then they left me to get on with it. I moved all of the furniture in their living room into the centre of the room, including the big old piano, which I then covered in dust sheets. All seemed to be going well. I did the walls, then began on the woodwork with a lovely deep blue gloss the owners had chosen. Painting the picture rail, I rested the tin of gloss on the piano. After I had finished the first coat, I went to move the tin and noticed with horror that a huge pool of blue paint had leaked through a hole in the dust sheet, and was already half set on the instrument's French-polished surface. I panicked. Instead of carefully trying to clean up my mess, I rubbed it off with sandpaper, ruining the surface forever. I then packed up my things and left, with the room half-painted, the piano a wreck, and a friend of a friend having to be avoided for the rest of my life.

HOLIDAY HIGH JINKS

HOTEL HORRORS
Tourist fouls up relationship

On the first night my girlfriend and I spent in our hotel in the USA, I
blocked the toilet and coated the bathroom floor in poo. Later that week,
after a heavy seafood and beer session, I started suffering a growling gut
that must have woken the place. Giving in to the call of the toilet, I
dropped my kecks seconds before the world fell out of my arse. I exited
the bathroom swiftly, to avoid being caught by the probable overflow that
would follow such a marathon session on the shitter. As I dived into bed,
I noticed that it was all hot and sticky: my arse had leaked all of its vile
contents during my drunken slumber! I grabbed a nearby bog roll, trying
to mop it up. But I'd wrought such anal devastation that my girlfriend's
leg was smeared in shit, and she was half-lying in a pool of foul-smelling
liquid. When a length of bog roll stuck to her leg and would not come off,
I returned, defeated, to the bog, upon which I fell asleep. I awoke to a
knock on the bathroom door, and my shit-smeared girlfriend, looking
terribly embarrassed, said, 'I'm really sorry, I think I had an accident.' My
male survival instincts kicked in, and I slyly countered, 'I know, that's why
I had to sleep in here all night.' To this day, although I remain justly proud
of the event, I cannot bring myself to tell her the truth.

LOVERS' TIFF
Man scares strange lady

A few years ago my then girlfriend and I decided to take a romantic break
in Paris. The day we set off we both found ourselves very highly strung
on the coach journey down to London. It was hot, the coach was
crowded, and we began to argue about halfway between Manchester and
Victoria. By the time we pulled in at London we were not speaking. My

girlfriend stormed off into a café, taking all of our money with her, while I stood outside and stewed. After about ten minutes I was furious. I burst into the café and stood behind my girlfriend ranting for a solid five minutes. I called her a selfish cow and shouted at the top of my voice, 'Now give me a bloody pound so I can buy myself a cup of tea!' At this point a girl I had never seen in my life turned around in tears and told me to please just leave her alone. My girlfriend, in an identical dress, was sitting two seats away laughing her head off.

NUDE NIGHTMARE
Camper puts on free show

I was hitch-hiking down the Californian coast when I stopped off at a camping resort, full of caravanning American families. It had been a long day on the road, and my only sustenance was some cheese and bottled water, so I decided to get some kip. I promptly fell asleep in my tent in the warm night. At about three in the morning, I awoke to hear a scratching noise, and in the beam of my torch I had the shock of my life to see several rows of gleaming teeth, as the local racoons availed themselves of my hospitality, I jumped, scared shitless, and started to run around my tent, yelling at the top of my voice to scare the buggers away. Unfortunately, the human residents of the campsite were also awoken, so I was illuminated by the lights of various caravans, family faces pressed against windows, as I gradually calmed down to a walking pace encircling my tent. Yes, it was hot. Yes, I was naked. Yes, I left the campsite that morning.

STILE SURPRISE
Rambler disturbs peer

Last summer I decided to go for a hike around Malham Cove in the Yorkshire Dales. Walking down to the footpath which would lead me to the cove, I could see, behind a stile, an elderly man crouching down, as if trying to catch his breath. Fearing the old soul might be in the grips of a coronary seizure, I increased my pace, thinking I might have to provide some emergency first aid. I sprinted the last hundred yards and vaulted over the stile, only to find that the old man wasn't having a heart attack at all. He was, in fact, having a pee. As I started to turn (to contain both our blushes), the old fellow turned to me with a huge smile. To my shock and amazement I realized he was none other than a prominent peer! I could do nothing but laugh as he offered an apology: 'Excuse me – I was only lubricating the way.'

HOLIDAY NEAR MISS
Drunk loses his way home

About three years ago, I was on holiday in Fuerteventura and on my first night there I got predictably drunk. Staggering home I got lost, but vaguely remembered there was a lighthouse near my hotel. Seeing a light in the distance I aimed towards it, and about an hour later I had to climb over a small fence. I was soon relieved to find myself on a tarmac road, and the lighthouse was now quite near. But my relief turned to sheer panic when I heard a huge roar just above me: I'd stumbled onto the runway of the airport, and the 'lighthouse' was in fact the control tower. A jumbo jet with its landing gear down shaved my head by no more than 20 feet, almost shattering my eardrums – and not doing my pants any favours either. When I finally made it home, I looked up the airport on my map. I'd gone about 12 miles off course.

HOLIDAY PRANK
Tourists end up in hospital

Heading out on holiday with 12 mates this summer, we expected a few disagreements between us, but didn't account on one individual who became universally hated. After a week of listening to his drivel, we decided to lose him out on the town, then get back early and lock the door, forcing him to climb over the partition from our neighbour's balcony. As we were only on the first floor we loosened the railings, just for good measure. Sure enough, just after two in the morning there was a bump as he fell, and we all ran out to hurl the usual insults. Apparently he landed harder than we expected, and suddenly rolled away down a little path leading to the sea. Springing into action, we all jumped down and chased after him, only for every one of us to run straight off the edge of a cliff. He landed on soft sand; we racked up three broken legs, two dislocated shoulders, two broken arms and serious cuts from a collection of broken glass and rusty cans.

NEAR DEATH EXPERIENCE
Holiday-makers meet bridge

While travelling around India, myself and a group of friends decided to sit on the roof of a bus for our short journey into town. Before too long we found that the previously crowded rooftop only held us four Brits. Where had all those Indians gone? Of course, unlike us, they had known. And – predictable I know – within minutes a low bridge loomed. Being slapped and stung by the overhanging coconut tree leaves had amused us, but a bridge took the piss. One friend peered over the side to seek help. The response? A giggling Indian. Another who was well positioned flew off the tail-end of the bus and held on to the ladder at the back. The rest of us had no chance. Fortunately, by ducking, there was a cool two-inch gap between life and a beheading.

ADULT PLEASURES
Tourists ogle centrefold

A few years ago, five mates and I headed out to Ibiza. Returning from the beach one day, we paused at the shops to get an evening's supply of beer. While two of the boys paid for the crate, the rest of us decided to check out the porn. One centrefold caught my eye – a girl being fisted by her lesbian mate, with two gentlemen giving her a damn good portion. I gave my mate a good elbow in the ribs and said, 'Here, look at this!' A weird silence followed. I looked up, and where I thought I'd flashed the sweat at my grinning chum, I'd just elbowed an elderly Spanish gent, who was now holding his ribcage and gasping for breath, as his wife covered her eyes – comedy style – with both hands. I was so shocked I just handed the mag to the wheezing old boy and walked out the shop.

CRUISER SLIPS
Drunken jig ends in disaster

A few years ago during a holiday in Mallorca, myself and six mates went on a booze cruise. After downing gallons of ale as our small vesel pootled round the bay, the boat anchored and my mates proceeded to dance on the deck. However, seeing their antics, the organizer warned everyone to be careful as it was very slippery. My mates duly stopped and sloped off for a swim, leaving me to finish my drink in peace. Soon I decided to join them and walked round the boat towards the steps which led into the sea, only to encounter a buxom lassie coming the other way. As we attempted to pass each other, I decided to make a joke of the situation and, grinning, began dancing like a constipated elephant. Of course, I immediately lost my footing and, as my feet went from beneath me, they connected with the girl's legs, drop-kicking her straight over the side and into the sea. We stuck to dry land from that day on.

HOLIDAY MEMENTO
Tourist cashes polaroid

Last year my fiancée and her friends decided to go to Cyprus for a holiday. As she would be gone a week, I took a Polaroid of myself (naked and sporting a massive stonker) to give her something to remember me by. When she returned I went to meet her at the airport, and before we went back home she decided to change the last of her foreign currency back into pound sterling. We eventually found the Bureau De Change and, without looking, she pushed a large wad of cash under the glass, along with the photograph of my erect knob, and asked, 'How much do I get for that?' Brilliantly, the female teller, who like me was crying with laughter, kept the picture, and gave me a wink when we left.

CRAB CHASED
Sea creature goes on the run

While on holiday in Ibiza, we decided to liven up our daytime activities with some masks and snorkels, and swimming out to see what we could uncover in San Antonio bay. Tying a large pebble to my underwater camera we would let it drop to the ocean floor, then race down to retrieve it. However, one of my friends became bored of the camera, and tied the rock to his 21st birthday present – a Rolex watch. It fell to the ocean floor without any problems, but just as we started to dive down, a huge crab scuttled over, grabbed it, waved his free claw triumphantly and headed off into deeper waters. My mate chased off after it, a torrent of swear words coming out of his snorkel. Finally, when he was almost out of sight, we heard a muffled, 'Fuck me, he's gone under a rock,' and almost had to be rescued as we were laughing too hard to swim. Needless to say, we bought him crab claws that night.

CARD TRICK
Nervous man makes crucial error

In 1999, I decided to check out Corfu with one of my mates. We booked into a hotel in a town called Sidari, and every night we donned our best clobber and headed out on the piss. On the fourth outing we bumped into an English rep, who was taking a group of holiday-makers on a pub crawl. She didn't mind us joining them, and by 3 am, as there was only her and I left, we went back to mine. Our clothes were off as soon as we got through the door. Then she looked me right in the eye and, in a husky voice, said

'Dominate me!' Unsure what to do, I nervously reached over and grabbed one of my adult playing cards. It was an eight of clubs, with a picture of a fat naked lady with her legs spread wide open. Holding it up in front of her, I said, 'See that? That's you!' She was out the door in three seconds flat.

DISASTER AT 20,000FT
Tourist in toilet trauma

Last Christmas I was on a overnight flight to the Gambia with my girlfriend and her parents who had kindly bought us a two-week break as a present. I was sitting in the aisle seat, with my prospective father-in-law opposite me. To break the ice, we shared a drink or two and it wasn't long before the large quantity I was consuming at altitude made me feel rather light-headed. As the lights in the cabin began to extinguish, there was no option but to adjourn to the little boys' room to relieve my bladder. I had mistimed badly and was leaking slightly as I tried to open the small door. I already had my flies undone and my old fella at the ready. As soon as I swung the door open, I rushed in, closed my eyes and enjoyed the immense pleasure that only such relief can bring. It then came to my attention that, instead of the delightful tinkling noise that I was expecting, there was more of a bass-like thud. It was too dark to see what was happening, so I finished what I had started and returned to my seat. When I next woke up I was dismayed to learn that there was to be no in-flight meal as the trolley which was kept in a room at the back had suffered a mishap.

HOT SHOT
Lovers face wrath of insomniac

My holiday in Mexico was going splendidly until an obnoxious American couple moved in next door. Every night they would keep us awake with their sexual marathons; loud slapping noises interjected with the occasional scream, groan and, on one occasion, the encouraging voices of another couple. Despite my complaints to the manager, the noise continued, so I decided to take matters into my own hands. Early one morning I got the wife to engage them in conversation while I dived over the balcony and doused the loud lady's bikini gusset with Mexican white pepper. Then we went to the swimming pool to await the results. Sadly, despite watching them swim for over an hour, nothing happened, and we retreated utterly defeated for another sleepless night. In the early hours of the morning, however, we suddenly heard a Yank voice announce: 'Gee honey, my cock is on fucking fire,' followed by an ear-piercing scream from his wife. Our only conclusion was that the pepper had somehow got inside her, and only made itself known once they had started shagging. We didn't get a peep out of them for the remaining four days.

COWBOY CAUGHT
Lover goes for ride

While travelling up the east coast of Australia, I spent a few days in a place called Airlie Beach with a young German girl. Our dorm had six people in it, so one night we left the bar early in an attempt to get some private time before the chaps returned. We had drunk a fair bit, and the result was that I simply couldn't shoot my bolt. Having tried several different positions, I spun her round and took her doggy style, but still no gentleman's gel. Boredom finally got the better of me, and I began to pretend I was a Rodeo cowboy, waving one hand in the air, while pretending to shoot charging Indians with the other. Mid shoot-out I noticed her staring at me in the full-length mirror next to the door, so I gave a sheepish wave, announced I was 'rather tired' and collapsed next to her. She never mentioned the incident.

TRAVELLER'S TRAUMA
Coach journey to nowhere

Just after leaving school, I spent several months travelling around South America. One morning, I boarded a crowded coach for what was to be a seven-hour journey, and took the seat at the back for a few hours' kip. Just before I dozed off, the driver jumped aboard, coughing and wheezing as he settled in for the journey. I must have been more tired than I thought because when I awoke and looked at my watch, six hours had passed. The bus had stopped, but on looking out of the window I saw that we were still in the same spot as when I had nodded off! The other passengers seemed OK about this, but I decided to find out what was going on, so I walked to the front and tapped the driver on the shoulder. To my horror, he pitched forward over the steering wheel. Apparently, his earlier coughing fit had been a heart attack, and he had died while everybody waited for him to start the journey.

BOTTLE-SMASHING FURORE
Tourists wind up french

I was staying on a French campsite with two friends. On our last night we got friendly with a couple of French girls and Dave, who spoke the language fluently. We all got very drunk and, at 5 am, there were a million broken beer bottles strewn across the campsite car park, but we just went to the beach to sleep it off. On our return to the scene we were greeted by a trio of irate Frenchmen – the owner of the campsite, the proprietor of a hotel whose guests had been kept awake all night, and a motorcycle cop. It was clear these Gauls were after our balls. Things were looking very *merde*-like when all of a sudden the cavalry arrived. Dave. He asked what the problem was and went off on the most passionate speech about ... what? We were clueless. When Dave stopped for breath, the Frenchmen looked at us with a sort of nostalgic fondness, smiled weakly, shook each of our hands and left. Apparently, we were grandsons of English war heroes who perished in the D-Day landings, here to celebrate the memories of our relatives in true English fashion – by raising a glass or a thousand, then smashing them all.

NUDE PHOTO SHAME
Tourist's vacation mishap

While travelling around Europe a few years ago, I ended up on the Greek island of Ios. Now Ios has the reputation of being a wild and outrageous resort, so after pitching our tent at the nearest campsite, my mate and I set off to explore. We trawled the bars and clubs and got absolutely leathered. The next morning I was woken by the distant giggle of women and the whirr of camera shutters. As I slowly came to, I realized I was lying on my back in the blazing sun. I tried opening my eyes, squinting at the blinding light, and lifting my medicine ball head to survey my surroundings. After a few minutes it all started coming back to me. I had indeed made it back to the campsite, but hadn't managed to get inside the tent, so after peeling off completely, I'd slept where I'd fallen. To my horror, I found that I'd been sleeping on my back, all morning, in front of the main entrance to the camp, bollock naked and with a hard-on like a blind cobbler's thumb. I've often wondered how many photo albums across the world my morning glory now adorns.

DRUG EXPORT FOLLY
Souvenir found at customs

A couple of years ago I was trekking in the Guyana rainforest with two friends when I chanced upon a particularly distinctive plant with five-fingered leaves. I plucked one of the leaves and pressed it between the pages of my passport. When the time came to leave Guyana, we packed our belongings and headed off to the airport. At passport control, I nonchalantly handed my passport to a very big, ugly Guyanan. As he flicked through it, the marijuana leaf, neatly pressed and dried, slid onto the desk. He looked up at me, and I contemplated a career change from medical student to prison inmate. Time stood still. Then, slowly, a smile began to creep across his face and he let out an almighty bellowing laugh. Catching on, I laughed as well, collected my passport and rejoined my friends. The leaf went into his pocket.

NAUTICAL HYGIENE WORRY
Makeshift tea urn scenario

Early morning on a cold Saturday about ten years ago, four artists, a printer, a photographer, an account executive and myself sailed five miles out from the Essex coast on a day's mission to catch a whopper. About 6.30 am I went in search of the loo, to be told in a roundabout way that all bodily functions were to be released over the side. At about eight, the skipper came topside with a fag in his mouth and a plastic washing-up bowl in his hands, containing eight cups of a piping hot drink and a plate full of sandwiches. Once finished, he collected the mugs and returned below deck. Within a couple of minutes he was back, yet again clutching the plastic bowl. He moved to the front of the boat and threw the contents of the bowl over the side. Seconds later a huge turd floated past our side of the boat. Bob, David and myself looked at each other in disbelief and burst out laughing. The thing was absolutely huge. Only the three of us had seen what had gone on, and within seconds of going down below the skipper emerged once again from his hole clutching the bowl with yet more food and drinks in it. The three on our side of the boat gave his menu a wide berth for the rest of the trip, while the five on the port side imagined they were getting preferential treatment.

MONKEY BOY SHOWS OFF
Drunkard scales incline

When I was 14, a few friends and I went camping near the top of a small (only 30 foot or so) cliff. After building a fire, we proceeded to get very drunk. As proof of my courage I drunkenly boasted that I would climb the cliff, overhang and all, without any equipment. At the base of the cliff I slipped and sprained my finger, but I'd had so much to drink it didn't hurt. I could feel my trainers slipping on the rock even at the start but I continued until I conquered the overhang and reached the top. Filled with elation I ran to tell my friends. They didn't believe me. I did it again, but this time with one of them sitting at the top of the cliff. As my head and arms came over the top of the overhang he started crying, saying: 'Don't fall, Huw. Please don't fall.' I couldn't help but laugh. I was holding onto the ledge with my feet dangling over the abyss, while my friend was sobbing drunkenly. I managed to pull myself together and get safely back onto the ledge, but I was badly frightened the next morning when I realized what I'd done.

AMSTERDAM SHOCKER
Drunk man shamed

Last year a group of us went to Amsterdam for the weekend for a beery break. On the first night we did the usual: got hammered and had a good look at the huge variety of strippers on show. Out of the six of us that were there one of my mates decided he was having too much of a laugh in the transvestite bar, and refused to come back to the hotel with the rest of us. At about five o'clock in the morning we heard him stagger into the hotel, causing a commotion as he banged his way along the corridor. By the time he got to our room we were all awake. He was completely bladdered and could not even talk. Within seconds of hitting the bed he was fast asleep, and it was then that the rest of us decided to wind him up. I spat into a condom, pulled down his pants, and poked the condom up his arse with a pen. Then we pulled his pants back up and left him to sleep. The next morning at breakfast we asked him how he had got on after we'd left, but he refused to talk. He stayed in his room for the whole day, claiming he was too hung-over to come out. That evening he also refused to join us. On the last day of our holiday we finally asked him if he had taken the condom out of his arse. He lost it. He dived across the table and punched me in the face. It took ages before he eventually saw the funny side.

BACK SCRATCHER
Swimmer meets reef dwellers

While on holiday in Phuket with my father, we decided to visit the island where the movie *The Beach* was filmed. For a few pence the locals would take you out over the coral, where you could dive down and feed the fish by hand, giving an amazing view of some big and colourful tropical species. Once in the water, some friends suggested to my dad that he pop a piece of bread between his teeth, and let the fish eat from his mouth. Amazingly, it worked, and we all marvelled at the shoal of little fish that swam bravely up to his chops to have a nibble. Then, suddenly, they all parted as a monster from the deep appeared from nowhere and snatched the entire bun from Dad's gob. The shock forced him to inhale a load of seawater, which promptly made him throw up his breakfast, and his whole body immediately disappeared as every creature on the reef, including crabs, descended on him. We had to leave him down there, floundering underwater, as we were laughing too hard to breathe.

SEASIDE HORROR
Men sleep on dead mammal

Several years ago, a group of friends and I set off on our motorbikes for a day in Great Yarmouth. After an uneventful trip, we hit the local hostelries, and six hours later decided to find a place to stay for the night. Unfortunately, as it was high season, most accommodation was fully booked and those places that weren't were unwilling to put up a dozen pissed bikers. Finally, most of us found places to stay, but two mates who were more pissed than the rest of us said they were going to crash out on the local beach. We arranged to meet up in the car park of a café at 9.30 am the next morning.

When we all met up as planned, the two lads who had slept on the beach turned up looking a bit sorry for themselves and stinking like a sewage farm. When asked what had happened, they told us that they had crashed on the beach at high tide, where they had found what they thought was a mound of tarpaulin. But when they woke that morning, they were horrified to discover that what had been keeping them warm all night was, in fact, the bloated carcass of a not-so-recently-deceased seal.

CAMP THUGS
Squealer dumped by gang

Back in the summer of 1992, I was participating in a Duke of Edinburgh Silver Award camping trip with several of my school friends. The trip was scheduled to last for three days, and on the first night a group of us decided to go to the village shop to get some beer. The night went well until one lad, who hadn't been invited to our shindig, blabbed to the teachers. We promptly got a bollocking and were threatened with expulsion if we did it again. Later that same night, when the grass was asleep in his bag, we tied belts around his arms and legs and gagged him with an old sock. We then carried him over a couple of fields and dropped him in one of those old wooden cow troughs. The water didn't cover him, so he lay in the few inches of mess at the bottom. We then went back to our tents, planning to pick the mug up a few hours later. At 6 am the next morning we were woken by our furious group leaders: the human slug had crawled across the fields inside his bag and turned up at camp. We were excluded from the award and made to buy the bastard a new bag.

DENTAL DISASTER
Laughing turk extracts tooth

Last year I went on holiday to Mersin in Turkey. Basically, the break was to be an eating and drinking extravaganza. The days blurred into one another and everything was going well on what was turning out to be the holiday of a lifetime, until disaster – I woke up one morning with a toothache which simply wouldn't go away. The agony proved so great that I had to go down to the hotel reception and explain to the bilingual girl behind the counter that I thought I was dying. She very kindly took me to a dental clinic: no moody affair with a rickety chair and a pair of pliers, but a professional-looking place. Anyway, the girl explained my dilemma. The dentist put me in the chair and looked into my mouth, then he injected my gum, making everything numb. Finally, and so quickly that I couldn't believe it had happened, he whipped my tooth out. I was stunned – and even more so when, cleaning out my mouth, he started to laugh. I asked the girl to translate for me and it turned out that, on closer examination, the dentist had realized I simply had a piece of garlic sausage stuck in my gum, and that the tooth hadn't needed to come out at all.

COUNTRY VIOLENCE
Lad clumped for beer error

Last summer, a friend and I decided to go on a bike ride into the countryside around Nottingham. After several hours of hard riding, we thought we should find a nice country pub and have a few pints to cool off. We walked into a pub full of villagers and local farmers, all of whom started to stare at us as we made our way to the bar. My friend got the drinks in as I nervously looked around the pub, trying to appear relaxed. For some reason, my eyes were drawn to the Guinness pump – the one shaped like a glass of the stuff. Taking anything to be a welcome distraction from the nasty looks I was getting from the other punters, I reached over to the pump and, to my horror, saw my fingers disappear into the head of a genuine pint of Guinness. The huge farmer at the bar whose pint it was didn't even let me finish the first word of an explanation: he smashed me to the floor immediately. Both my friend and I were then physically ejected from the pub without getting a sip of drink.

TRAVELLER WELCOMED
Wrong number blunder

Two years ago I was on a solo trip around the world, bunking on the floors of relatives and friends whenever I could. While in Jakarta I was quite keen to get in touch with Peter – a friend of my brother – who had offered to put me up during my stay in London. Finally I managed to get through, only to be told by his flatmate that unfortunately Pete had been beaten up. He was in hospital for a few days, and his flatmate, Shane, told me I was welcome to stay in his absence. I had a brilliant week, and on the Friday Peter's mum dropped him off, whereupon I introduced myself as Troy's brother. From behind a busted nose, a confused Pete mumbled 'What? I don't know a Troy.' Somehow I had managed to call the wrong flat that contained another Pete. They kindly let me stay a night, but I left the next day.

TOILET TROUBLE
Hiker makes new friend

Last summer a friend and I went on a walking holiday in Snowdonia. As we were using up lots of energy, we ate high fibre foods such as pasta and potatoes, which obviously led to long toilet sessions. One of the campsites had a stand-alone toilet block, complete with showers, and I was sitting there one evening doing my business when I happened to glance up and see a skylight directly above me. In its reflection I could see the tiled floor just outside my cubicle. After wiping, I stepped out and looked up again, and sure enough I could see back inside the bog. Not only that, but I could see down into every other cubicle as well – including the bloke two down, who was still having a dump. Just as I was wondering what sort of pervert had designed such a feature, the bloke looked up, and our eyes locked. Sheepishly, I gave him a little wave, and then legged it back to my tent, from where I watched him stalk around the site for a full hour, looking for me.

FAT PUDDING
Man grabs wrong meal

Last summer I went to Florida for a holiday with my wife and parents. While there, we all went to a buffet-style restaurant where you could eat as much as you like. The food wasn't particularly fancy, so we were very surprised when my dad sat down with a huge knickerbocker glory. When we asked where he'd got it from, he said it was from the dessert stand. Our waiter then approached and asked if we were okay. Thirty seconds later he returned with the same question, paying close attention to my father. Then he asked him if he would like to choose another dessert. Dad was almost half-way through the monstrous delight, so he said no. The waiter then patiently explained that the ice-cream was for display purposes only, and was in fact made out of – what we would call in England – lard. Apparently it was several months old, and was put in the freezer every night to keep its shape.

GIFT DELIVERED
Red face for souvenir hunter

During an all-boys holiday in Magaluf in 1999 my mate, Keato, managed to pull a nice-looking girl, and took her back to the apartment. In the morning we piled into his room for the lowdown on his night of action. 'Did you get some, then?' I demanded. 'Yep,' he replied, 'and she clearly loved every minute of it as she's left me a souvenir.' He then disappeared into the bedroom and returned with a pair of yellow knickers. 'Smell that, lads, it's the sweet smell of pussy!' he gloated. And then Dave announced, 'Actually, they're my dirty pants.'

FOREIGN FIASCO
Traveller has toilet trouble

I had been cooped up with seven people on a sailing holiday around the Greek islands on a 38 ft (11.5 m) yacht for two weeks. After a long, hot day at sea, we entered a harbour to moor up and relax for a few days. I was feeling the urge to splurge, but discovered that nobody had emptied the bilge tank. As the toilet became unusable for the next two days, a friend and I trekked off into the town and found a bar with a toilet. By now, I was facing the biggest evacuation since *Towering Inferno*. I opened the door to find a pan in an area big enough to swing a kitten. There was no light, window or lock. I called to my mate and asked him to stand guard. By leaving the door open and keeping my foot against it to make a one-inch gap, I had just enough light to allow me to place my bare behind on the seat. But when it came time to wipe up, it wasn't possible to maintain the gap in the door without it swinging open, so I shut it. I was now in complete darkness. I fumbled around until I placed my hand on some paper – and pulled. Now, you must understand that this was my first time in Greece and I didn't realize that when disposing of used toilet paper, due to their poor sewage system, they put it into a bin. I was pulling at someone else's waste! Not unsurprisingly, the closest I ever go to Greece now is a chicken kebab on a Friday night.

DESPERATE MEASURES
Stewardess gets nasty shock

I was recently in Kefalonia, where the drainage system is so poor that a single flush of the toilet is woefully inadequate. On the last day we went out to the airport, where I was suddenly hit by serious stomach cramps. I found a secluded toilet just in time, releasing a ferocious explosion that reverberated around the room. The stench was eye-watering, and to make matters worse, the flush was broken. As I strolled out, however, I walked straight into two air stewardesses doing their make-up in the mirror. I was in their rest room, but after their initial shock they saw the funny side, and promised not to tell. Then without warning, one of them walked into the cubicle. There was the briefest of pauses followed by an ear-deafening screech, at which point I sheepishly bolted for the plane, not even slowing down for customs.

HOLIDAY HORROR
Piss-head pranks

Going on your summer holiday is supposed to be a time of non-stop joviality, drinking and shagging. So, last year I went on holiday with five mates to Tenerife. Naturally, we started our celebrating as soon as the plane left London. We drank all through the flight, and continued chucking it back through our first night on the island. In the morning we were quite shattered and went down to the beach with a few beers to recuperate. After a few cans of lager I fell asleep and woke up some four hours later in great agony. I rushed to the local hospital and was given some cream and told to stay out of the sun for the next few days. Gutted, I returned to my hotel room. And only then did the full horror of my situation hit me. Looking in a mirror for the first time I was shocked to see the word 'WANKER' written on my forehead in sun protection factor 30 by my 'mates' as I slumbered on the sand.

SURPRISE CUISINE
Lover dishes out revenge

About four years ago I fell in love with a beautiful Lebanese girl, and after
a whirlwind romance she took me to Lebanon to meet her family. Sadly,
I couldn't help but ogle at the multitude of tanned women strutting
around wearing very little, so before long we were having blazing rows
and I was sleeping on the sofa. Finally she suggested that we make our
peace, and offered to take me for a delicious Arabian lunch. I agreed, and
although I took great pains to avoid the raw meats and liver, I couldn't
get enough of the sliced potato in lemon sauce she offered me. It was
delicious, and I ate three plates of the stuff over the course of two hours.
After the feast we went for a stroll along the beach, and it was then that
my girlfriend burst out laughing, and mockingly revealed that the potato
was in fact sheep's testicles. With two weeks and 28 meals of my stay
in Lebanon remaining, I decided not to even glance at another woman.

FILTHY TOSSER
Man caught out by spanish glass

Three mates and I went to Ibiza for two weeks. A few days into the
holiday, three of us were sitting by the hotel pool when some girls came
over and asked if we were in the flat overlooking the main road. When
we said we were, they laughed and said we'd better hang a towel across
the window – which went from floor to ceiling and appeared frosted from
the inside – because it was totally clear from the café across the road and
everybody could see us showering. Slightly embarrassed, we made our
way back to the flat. Later on that evening our fourth friend, who hadn't
heard about the window, went to have his shower. We thought it would
be a laugh not to tell him about the 'view' and went across to the café,
pointing out the spectacle to fellow holiday-makers. Imagine our horror
as our mate started to have a wank. Worse still, he put the shower head
to unusual and good effect. After all manner of contortions I thought
enough was enough, and knocked on the bathroom door and told him
to stick his head out of the window. When he did he was greeted with
a loud cheer from the crowd below, and he spent the rest of the holiday
refusing to leave the apartment.

MISTAKEN IDENTITY
Australian makes stars appear

Many years ago, after being bored rigid by friends' tales of foreign adventure, my mate Nigel and I went to Australia to see what all the fuss was about. We ended up in Bondi, and one afternoon we were walking home when Nigel nudged me and pointed out the British actor Terence Stamp. I knew it was him, but for no real reason, I said he looked nothing like Mr Stamp, and teased him all the way home, pointing at people with moustaches and shouting, 'Look, Burt Reynolds!' He finally snapped, and marched back to find our great actor. We found him sitting in the window of a local café, minding his own business with a coffee and paper. 'See, it is him,' said Nigel triumphantly, but I just laughed and said Terence had bigger ears. Terence couldn't help but notice two men pointing at him through the glass, and he started to look rather irate. Nigel then started stopping people in the street to get their opinion, even going so far as to knock loudly on the glass, until Stamp could take no more. He sprinted out the door, and it wasn't until he was within a yard of us that we realized two things: he wanted a fight, and it wasn't Terence Stamp. Suffice to say, Nigel had the shit kicked out of him by Australia's best look-alike.

SKI ACCIDENT
Holiday-maker cut short

A few years ago I went on a skiing holiday with friends to a resort in Switzerland. On the first day we caught the cable car, and at the top of the mountain one of the girls in our group decided that she needed to pee. The only available loo was in a terrible condition however, and she convinced herself that she could hold on until she reached the bottom of the slopes. About 300 yards down the hill she realized that she had been wrong, and we waited for her as she promptly skied off into the woods that ran down the left side of the run. Trying to be as quick as possible, she decided against removing her skis, opting instead to simply drop her saloppetes, crouch down, and hold onto an overhanging branch. We then heard a loud snap as the branch broke, and could only watch in awe as she came bombing out of the shrubbery, naked from the waist down with her trousers around her ankles, and clutching the remnants of a branch.

The lift station was about 50 yards below her, and she crashed into about 500 people standing patiently in the queue. Although they all saw the funny side, she spent the rest of the holiday hiding in the hotel.

SEXUAL SHENANIGANS

MOBILE MISTAKE
Texting lothario makes do

Not long ago, I met a girl in an internet chat-room. We got on well, so she gave me her mobile number and asked me to call. We exchanged a few texts, then a few days later she sent me a really filthy suggestion. I tapped in a suitable reply, searched through my address book for her name, and sent it. Her reply seemed a little strange but I didn't think anything more of it, as we were soon exchanging even more explicit texts. Eventually we decided to meet at a hotel, but when I got there at the appointed time who was there but my cousin. I said 'hi' and was about to ask what she was doing at the hotel, when it hit me; my cousin and the girl I'd originally been chatting to have the same first name, and both their numbers were stored in my phone. I didn't really know what to do, but my cousin's pretty attractive … so I went through with it with her instead.

DOOR SLAMMER
Toilet becomes peep booth

Four years ago while attending college in Northern Ireland, myself and my girlfriend decided that we would take a week off college to visit both of our parents. As we settled into our train seats, it suddenly dawned on me that we would have to wait seven long days before having sex again, so I suggested that we nip off to the train toilet for a quick shag. I thought my woman would say no, but amazingly she agreed, and it wasn't long before we were both half-naked and I was slamming her doggy-style over the little sink. Just as I let rip up her back, I heard a cough behind me, and we turned to discover that, in our haste, we hadn't shut the door properly, giving the entire carriage a free porn show. To make things worse, the train was packed, and we had to stand for two and a half hours with everyone grinning and winking at us.

PRIVATE EDUCATION
Darkness confuses student

In 1997, when I was still in the upper-sixth at school, several French student teachers arrived for teacher training. One night they all turned up in our local pub, and I ended up pulling one of the better-looking ladies of the group. After that, our relationship continued during school hours, every day at 4.10 pm in the language lab. After three days of complete success, I decided to arrive a few minutes early to get a head-start on things. To my horror, the next person to arrive was the head of modern languages – an old, chalk-haired duffer who looked stunned to find a naked lad in the darkened room muttering, 'I wanted you so much in class today.' Desperate to keep my girl out of trouble, I chose an excuse that I regret to this very day. I told the old fool that I was confused, and had strange feelings for him. No more was said, but I was dumped two days later for another teacher.

DIRTY-TALK DISASTER
Sexual ignorance exposed

I was out with my mates in the local nightclub, when a horny babe came up to me on the dancefloor and started talking really dirty. Astounded by my good fortune, I left my pint and my mates and disappeared outside with her. While searching for a suitable spot to do the dirty deed, I came across a secluded path surrounded by bushes. Perfect. Within seconds we were in the throes of passion, she whispered, 'Put me on the cross, put me on the cross.' Thinking she was moaning to herself, I carried on, but moments later she moaned again, 'Put me on the cross.' Baffled by her rambling, I still carried on regardless. Minutes later, she moaned even louder, 'Put me on the cross.' By now I was beginning to think she knew some sexual position I didn't. Not wanting to appear incompetent, I grabbed her arms, pinned them at right angles to her body, put her legs together so she was in the shape of a crucifix, and kept on pumping. 'What the hell are you doing?' she cried. 'Putting you on the cross,' I said confidently. She replied, 'I said to put me on the *grass*, these bloody stones are hurting my back.'

LIVE SEX IN SOHO
Exhibitionists in the dark

I had been pursuing a dark beauty from Sierra Leone for several months. Her defences eventually came down and we became a couple. I decided, one weekend, to treat her to a West End show and then a meal in Soho. In the restaurant, we got closer and closer, touching parts of each other that shouldn't really be touched in public … So, we paid the bill and escaped quickly, scrabbling over the fence into the garden in the middle of Soho Square for a bit of privacy. On a patch of grass, we started to kiss and grope each other. Before we knew it, we were buck naked and humping away. We were loving every minute of it, but, unfortunately our attention was focused on each other and not on the crowd of men from a nearby gay bar who had gathered to watch. Once we realized what was going on, my girlfriend and I really got off on all the attention we were getting. However, we didn't realize that, due to my girlfriend's colour, our audience couldn't see her in the dark. Only my big white butt was visible, as it furiously moved up and down on the grass. Presumably, the various characters from the bar thought I was having sex with a hole in the ground.

SEASIDE SHAG
Couple have filthy sex

It was to be a romantic weekend away for myself, my girlfriend and another couple. We drove up to Hunstanton on a hot summer's day, parked the car and set off along the beach with our provisions: plenty of drink and some food for cooking on the driftwood fires we planned to build. We set up camp, sipped red wine and ate sausages cooked in cider as the sun went down. The tide drifted out, and the moon rose as the fire slowly died. My mate and his girl went for a walk, while I decided to hit the hay with my new love. We walked back up the beach to a row of beach huts, giggling all the while, and broke into one. We drunkenly fell to the floor and had a great sweaty sex session, before falling into deep slumber. In the morning I woke up and curiously patted the crunchy floor of the cabin with my hands. My girlfriend did the same. As my mate swung the door open and sunlight bathed the room, we were all disgusted to see that we had spent our night of passion on a carpet made up of millions of dead flies.

CHRISTMAS LIGHTS
Woman puts everything on display

When my mother-in-law first bought her flat, my wife and I went to spend a Christmas with her. The sleeping arrangements were tight to say the least, and we found ourselves kipping in a large sleeping-bag on the living room floor. As usual, the missus was feeling horny at the idea of sleeping in a strange place and we spent the night hard at it. In the morning she got up to use the bathroom, when suddenly the hall lights went on, and the door started to open. Attempting to dive back under the covers, the wife stumbled over my outstretched leg, shot along the smooth fabric of the sleeping-bag and, to my complete amazement, tipped head first into the Christmas tree, giving my entering mother-in-law and her 13-year-old nephew a splendid view of her own, personal, decorations.

CAUGHT IN THE ACT
The dog gets it

One summer I was at a mate's house revising for impending exams. Having spent several hours studying intensively, we were both in need of a break. My mate suggested we reward our hard work by watching one of his brother's porno videos. Within minutes of watching an on-screen orgy, my teenage libido was in overdrive and I needed a wank. Casting an eye across the room, I could see my mate was thinking the same. Not wanting to miss any action, I simply put my hand down the front of my trousers. After ten minutes, my attention was drawn to movement out of the corner of my eye. To my utter horror, my mate's mum had returned home early and was making her way towards the back door. I froze as she looked in through the patio doors, pointing at us with her mouth wide open. 'How many times have I warned you about this,' she bellowed as she entered the lounge. 'I've told you time and time again, you'll get hairs all over the furniture!' I was about to make my excuses when she interrupted. 'Don't let Sandy on the furniture!' she bellowed. Then, with immense relief, the penny dropped. Somehow she had looked straight past the two of us abusing ourselves and had spotted Sandy, the border collie, sitting on a chair at the far end of the room.

AVON CALLING!
Gent's lubricant horror

A few years ago, I pulled a 'naughty forty'. She didn't need much persuading to accompany me back to my mother's house, where I was living. During the early stages of foreplay, she left me in no doubt as to what she would like me to do to her … I can't explain in full, as I'm led to believe it may still be illegal in this country. I left the bedroom and stumbled to the bathroom without turning on the light, so as not to disturb my mother sleeping in the adjacent room, I returned with a pot of the best lubricant I could find and applied it liberally to the appropriate areas. Ten minutes into my routine, I noticed a distinct chafing that I'd never experienced before. But I saw the job through to the end and was soon kipping soundly. Imagine my horror when I awoke in the morning to discover my manhood looking as if it had been dipped in concrete and my mum's Avon face-mask next to the bed.

WASHING MACHINE WOE
Kitchen sex curtailed

I was once seeing a girl who was renting a room in a house where the washing machine was always breaking down. Whenever her housemate was out, we grabbed the opportunity to make love, and often didn't even make it to the bedroom in our passion. One morning, my girlfriend had agreed to stay in as a man was coming round to fix the washing machine once and for all; we had waited days for an appointment and of course, he hadn't turned up the first time he promised to. We were in the kitchen when we started kissing. After about 30 seconds we were both minus our clothes and using the worktop for our enjoyment. This became a screaming session and most of the screaming came from me. In the (occasional) quiet moments, I could dimly hear voices – I thought it was the TV – and suddenly I saw someone walking through the lounge towards the kitchen. We froze for a moment, then both grabbed what we could and tried to get dressed. But it was going to be too late. Panicking, I walked into the lounge, stark bollock naked, holding a pile of clothes and shouted back into the kitchen without thinking, 'Darling, can you get the rest of the clothes out of the washing machine, they're done.' The plumber looked me up and down in a bemused way and said, 'Has it been fixed? I'll be going then.'

SEX-IN-PUBLIC SHAME
Couple caught in the act

My girlfriend and I had been out clubbing on a Saturday night and were heading home. On the way, I went to a cashpoint to get some money. It was one of those where the machine is in a foyer inside the bank. While I was completing my transaction, my girlfriend started fondling me from behind. One thing led to another and soon I had her up against the wall and we were going at it like rabbits. After our unexpected passion, we slipped out and thought nothing more of it ... until the Monday morning. The big news in the paper was that there had been a spate of vandalism in the city centre on the Sunday morning. One of the damaged buildings was the very bank that had been the scene of nocturnal passion. According to the report, the bank was planning to run through the security video from the foyer to see if they could find any clues ...

A TASTE OF LOVE
No cure for hangovers

After I'd wined and dined my newish girlfriend, we decided on a drink back at my pad, with a side-serving of rumpy-pumpy. Before I could even finish my bottle of beer, we headed for the bedroom and, after a hefty session, fell asleep, exhausted. I woke up with that post-drinking binge 'ashtray' mouth and, seeking to quench my thirst, spotted the unfinished bottle of beer. It was infinitely more appealing than crawling over to the kitchen, so I took a swig. It tasted flat and disgusting, as if someone had put a fag out in it, but I polished it off. Later, I asked my still-dozing girlfriend, 'Did you put something in my beer last night?' She looked at me in sympathy. 'Remember how I said I don't swallow? Well, I had to put it somewhere …'

WET SHEET MISJUDGMENT
Tomato soup leads to more bladder shame

A few years ago, after a particularly good Friday night session with the lads, I remember getting into a taxi with a young lady just before I fell into an alcohol-induced coma. I awoke some hours later, alone in a double bed in a strange room. I got out of bed to get dressed when I realized my clothes had gone. I went to the bedsit door and called out, but no-one seemed to be in the building. 'Oh shit, I've been rolled,' I thought, and determined to wreak vengeance by pissing over the double bed. I had just begun to do so, when in walked said young lady with my clothes. They were washed and ironed as I'd managed to throw tomato soup all over myself in the cab.

PULLING TRICKS
Lady offers over the odds

A few years ago my wife and I decided to go out for a large night in Paisley, and as such, the missus was kitted out in a very sexy miniskirt and high white boots. As we walked down the street deliberating where to go, my wife stopped to look in the window of an estate agents. Suddenly, out of nowhere, an older man appeared and said quite openly, 'How much?' Still looking at the properties and not paying much attention, my wife replied '£48,000'. The old boy replied in disbelief, 'How much?' Then, just when I thought things couldn't get any funnier, she explained, 'Yes, but that's for a semi.'

WHORE'S BATH
Costly wipe-down

A few years ago I made it my aim in life to pull the gorgeous Irish barmaid in my local, and after several weeks' flirting I finally asked her out. Not only did she say yes, but the rest of the night went so well that she invited me back to her house. After snogging in the taxi, we arrived at hers. As she went to the toilet I was left in a bit of a panic: I hadn't showered that morning. As things were going so well it seemed only a matter of minutes before my old fella would be brought into action, so I crept into the darkened kitchen and gave myself a bit of a clean 'south of the border' with a handy flannel. She soon returned and, sure enough, we got straight down to it, with me lying on the couch while she went down on me. But no sooner had her lips touched my bits than she straightened up. 'What's that?' she asked, pointing to my pubes. On inspection I saw a solitary baked bean nestled among the curly hairs – the 'flannel' I'd used had, in fact, been a dirty dishcloth. I left red-faced and never saw her again.

TENTING DISGUISED
Lover stuns prospective in-laws

One Sunday my mate Steve and his fiancée drove to the local garden centre with her parents. During the trip, his good lady started touching him up on the back seat and her fingers soon had the desired effect. Once they arrived at the centre, Steve realized that as the car had no back doors, he would have to take great care exiting the vehicle in order to hide his obvious excitement. When his mother-in-law to be opened the door and pulled the seat down he executed a smooth, half-crouching manoeuvre, before turning swiftly and marching off towards the plants. Relieved that he had escaped a potentially embarrassing situation, he was then stunned to hear a familiar voice on the other side of the conifers exclaim: 'Did you see the size of his hard-on, Frank? I thought he was going to have my bloody eye out.'

UNWELCOME SURPRISE
Birthday boy gets caught out

My friend, an airman, had his 21st birthday a few weeks before being posted to Saudi Arabia. His parents asked if he would like a big party to celebrate. He declined the offer, asking instead if he could have a quiet evening at home with his girlfriend, cook her a meal, candles, soft music – and, while his parents were out, a good sex session to keep him going for the four months he'd be away. So, the night came, his parents went out, and a fine meal was prepared. The wine flowed and eventually the pair were rolling around the living room in their favourite position: the 69. While in full swing the phone rang. 'Let's answer it in this position,' my friend suggested, and off they wriggled into the hall. It was his mother on her mobile. 'Your dad thinks he's left his glasses in the kitchen, can you check, please,' she said. Once again, he suggested they stay in the position. 'It'll be a laugh,' he said. Off they wriggled again, laughing all the way. 'Surprise, surprise! Happy birthday!' was their greeting as they opened the door. And, of course, Mum, Dad, Grandma, aunties, uncles and cousins were all there to congratulate the young man, bless them.

GROUP-SEX CRINGER
Sucker comes a cropper

A booze-sodden evening at the nightclub was shaping up very nicely indeed when my cousin Steve and I pulled Sarah and Lindsey, two pert 18-year-olds, and brought them back to my pad. Dispensing with all our clothes, and making the best of a bad deal (I only had one bed), all four of us ended up sharing, and enjoying it loads. In the throes of passion I reached over and started sucking his bird (Lindsey's) nipples. The next day the girls were up and out early on, leaving Steve and me to compare notes on the team acrobatics. We both enjoyed going over my cheeky nuzzling of Lindsey's breasts, but Steve remained strangely quiet when I mentioned that she seemed to have flaky skin on her tits. Then he revealed that he didn't have a condom, so he'd just shot his load over her front and then rubbed it in. My mouth suddenly went very dry as the penny dropped and I realized that her 'dry skin problem' didn't actually involve dry skin.

RUSTIC LOVERS
Anglers enjoy free show

Last summer my girlfriend and I spent a glorious day on the banks of a loch in northern Scotland. Having enjoyed our picnic and a couple of bottles of chilled Chardonnay, we both became very horny. I had the bright idea of setting up the tent early for a bit of afternoon sex, and we crawled inside for a long, drawn-out session. We stayed inside for a couple of hours, running through a variety of positions and thoroughly enjoying ourselves in the fresh Scottish air. Eventually I got dressed and climbed out of the tent for a late afternoon ciggie. On my emergence I saw two fishermen sitting in a rowboat at the shore of the loch. I said hello and they smiled at me, waved, and rowed away. I looked back up at the tent and saw that, due to the setting sun, our tent was totally transparent, and the anglers had obviously had a perfect view of my girlfriend and I going through our contortions.

RADIO EXPOSURE
Student DJ goes bonkers for bingo

While at university a few years ago, I was fortunate enough to land a slot on the campus radio. It was a position I turned to my advantage to cultivate an image of hip and coolness – which surprisingly pulled the girls. I would often taken my conquests back to the studio, which I used as a secret shag pad. One evening, I took a girl back there and we started messing about with a bingo game which the station used. We called out the numbers and took our clothes off as a forfeit. Eventually we were both butt-naked as I pulled out a final fake forfeit, which said 'Spread your legs and think of England.' There then ensued a frantic bout of shagging, culminating in the girl shouting, 'House! Bingo!' while in the throes of ecstasy. The following day, we were mortified when walking around campus as fellow students pointed and nudged, with cries of 'Bingo!' It seems I'd inadvertently knocked the broadcast switch on during our high jinks and some community-spirited listener had informed as many people as he could.

BACK SCRATCHER
Mother discovers electrical toy

A couple of months ago, while unpacking following a dirty weekend in Amsterdam, my girlfriend came across a large vibrator that we had purchased while we were there. Within minutes the sparks of Holland were flying in our living room, when there was a loud knock at the door. It was her mother, who had popped round to see the holiday snaps, so after a frantic scramble to hide the toy and put some clothes on, we let her in and settled down in front of the television. Then, right in the middle of *Blind Date*, her mum whips out the vibrator from behind a cushion, looks at it closely and announces, 'Ooh, your sister's got one of these.' Apparently, the crafty cow had claimed that the plastic purple monster was a totally innocent back massager, and I sat there utterly speechless while the old crone sighed with obvious pleasure and started rubbing her neck with the very same electrical appliance that had only recently been right up her daughter's jacksie.

POST-SHAG COCK-UP
Humiliation in station

Last summer, I caught up with an old flame and ended up having a totally unexpected night of passion. Alas, the only suitable venue was the lounge floor of her parents' house. In the morning, despite having had no sleep, I had my wits about me and, being a decent chap, I secreted the now full (but tightly knotted) condom on my person, rather than have her mother find the dried version some months later behind her sideboard. Being stranded some miles from my house in the bright morning glare and with about £2 left from the night before, I selected public transport as the best route home. With thoughts now centred on a very long sleep, I joined the queue at the train station to purchase my ticket. Imagine the look of horror on the face of the woman behind the window when I innocently delved into my pocket and brought out not only the correct change but a thoroughly well-used condom. She advised me to buy my ticket on the train.

EATING IN BED
Love nugget

Stone me if I wasn't sitting at a table for two with a babe! Not wanting to seem the gannet by ordering a 12 oz steak, I settled for the lighter option of a tuna and sweetcorn pasta plus a couple of glasses of house red. A few bottles later and we're talking about this, that ... and the other. She soon invited me back to her place for the other. Game on! We moved from position to position, until we got to number 69 when a distinct rumble from my stomach informed me of an imminent bum eruption. Clenching my buttocks but at the point of no return, I climaxed and passed wind simultaneously. To my horror, out popped a single knob of corn, smiling up at me from the black silk sheets. My mother always told me to chew my food. I'm just grateful I didn't have the fruit cocktail.

OFFICE SEX
Coffee cream

Recently I decided to start seeing a work colleague. Bearing in mind that I work in an office with over 20 females and only two males, my years of office celibacy were highly commendable – or stupid! So one Sunday, said colleague and I were working hard, when she challenged me to a bout of shagging round the office! Always up for a challenge, I duly obliged. After 45 minutes' worth of some of the best nookie I've ever had, it was time to cover our tracks. We had, however, left a 'wet patch' on one desk and, agonizingly, there was not a jot of toilet paper in the whole damn office. Using our initiative, we grabbed a tea towel, wiped up and made tracks home! Imagine my horror the next day when, with clients arriving at 9.15 am, a secretary was wiping the cups with the same towel we'd used not 12 hours earlier. My guilt was further increased when the client noted a peculiar taste on the rim of his cup! The towel, which had an oddly musky smell, was identified as the culprit. No-one could identify this odour; the offending item was sent for a wash and the client given a clean cup.

BATHROOM SHOCKER
Shag brings out firemen

When I was a student I lived in a 'mixed' household, which thankfully meant that the boys and the girls all lived together. My girlfriend at the time was a lively lass, and liked to experiment sexually. With this in mind she arranged for us to have a sexy bath together one evening when all the other students were out 'studying'. We lit the draughty old bathroom with candles which we rested on the window sill, filled the bath to the brim with bubbles, and slipped into the water for some serious cleansing. Suddenly, just as I was soaping some interesting body parts, and having some of mine vigorously rubbed clean, there was a thundering crash at the door, followed by loud shouting. Two security guards were battering down the door with fire extinguishers. After a few seconds of stunned silence from both sides they started to piss themselves with laughter. It seems they had been patrolling the grounds near our house and had seen a 'massive fire' in one of our windows. Our flickering candles, through the frosted glass, had led them to storm in on our sexy bubble-bath. After they had left we couldn't quite recreate the atmosphere, so the whole night was a write-off.

VIDEO EXPOSURE
Waitress relieves barman

Years ago, I worked in a hotel during my summer holidays. The place only had one till, and this was shared between the bar and the restaurant. There was a lot of pilfering. As it was used by so many members of staff, it was very hard for the management to find out who had the sticky fingers, so they decided to install a security camera to catch the culprits. At the end of the first session with the new equipment we were all called into the office to watch as our boss fast-forwarded through the tape. This boring task produced no evidence at all, and we were all just about to fall asleep when, on the screen, one of the waitresses, clearly getting a bit carried away with the task of kissing one of the barmen goodnight, dropped to her knees and gave him a very expert blow job – much to our amusement. The video tape still survives to this day, and works perfectly well as a training video for new staff members.

LODGER KNOCKED UP
Feline ensures rage

My girlfriend and I first started having sex when she lived with her father. We didn't hear him come in one night, and he embarrassed us the next morning with a stern lecture on the subject of manners and not having sex under his roof. We left things for a while, but tried again after a night on the piss, only to be met in the morning with the words, 'This is the last time I'll tell you, boy.' Finally, after my company's Christmas party I decided not to risk it and slept in the spare room. During the night the cat tried to get in, and commenced a rhythmic scratching at the door. This lasted a few minutes, until a furious voice bellowed out: 'Stop fucking my daughter!'

FIRST DATE HORROR
One-night stand is off-colour

I was working in Edinburgh as a nightclub manager a few years ago, and one evening a gorgeous girl came up to me and asked me if I would like to go out with her the following night. I couldn't believe my luck and shared my good news with two of the club's bouncers, Steve and Tom. The following night I was changing in the club and getting excited about my big date. Suddenly Tom and Steve came in, held me down and poured green food colouring all over my bollocks. As I was only minutes away from my date, I let the stuff dry, got dressed and went to meet Jackie. We had a great evening: a meal with some wine, some dancing with plenty of drinks, and she invited me back to her place. We got down to some drunken shagging and I fell asleep a very contented man. I was woken at 7 am by Jackie screaming. She was standing in front of the mirror: her face was green, her tits were green, her hands were green and her thighs were green. She had to take the day off work and never spoke to me again.

TRAINEE FIREMAN
Passion causes inferno

A few years ago I was seeing a young girl who still lived with her parents. Every Thursday evening I would go round to her house and disappear upstairs with her to 'play on her PC'. This particular evening she had some perfumed candles littered around the place, and we got straight down to things. I kept the groans to a minimum so that her parents wouldn't become suspicious, and after we had finished I slipped off the condom, dropped it in the bin, and snuggled back up with my girl. It was then that I noticed the smell of burning and realized that one of the candles had set fire to the bin's contents – basically a load of tissues and a used rubber johnny. As I leapt out of bed, I accidentally kicked the contents across the room, and we suddenly had a serious fire on our hands. So naked as the day I was born, I heroically grabbed the nearest thing – a 10-inch (25-cm) rubber dildo that we used for foreplay – and began beating the carpet furiously. And then her father burst through the door shouting, 'What's all the noise about up here?' Needless to say, I took advantage of his few moments of shocked disbelief, grabbed my trousers and legged it, pausing only once to throw a blackened plastic cock into their hedge.

CHUBBY CHASER
Man gets mouthful

A while ago, after more than a few delicious beverages at my local I pulled a rather large woman, and persuaded her to let me go back to her house when the pub shut. We soon got down to business, and despite the room being pitch black, it wasn't hard to locate her massive boobies, so I started sucking greedily on a hardened nipple. And then, rather surprisingly, I got a gob full of warm milk. Being the perfect gentleman, I immediately asked her if she had recently given birth, but she rather testily claimed that she hadn't. So I carried on regardless and had a thoroughly enjoyable night of blubber-bashing with the chubby goer. When I woke in the morning I looked down at the beached whale and was rather horrified to see, about half an inch from her nipple, the shrivelled remains of a monstrous boil which I had clearly sucked dry during our night of passion.

ART APPRECIATION
Romantic holiday ruined by sex

Last summer I rented a villa on the Canary Islands with my girlfriend and her parents. It was situated right on the beach front and, one hot evening, the lovely romantic setting had us feeling a little saucy, so the love of my life led me down to the sand for some sexual activity. Things were going great, but as I took her doggy style she looked over her shoulder and grumpily shouted, 'Do me harder, you ginger tosser!' Devastated, I stopped, and headed back to the house to sleep alone on the sofa. Things got much worse at breakfast however, when her mother haughtily told us that during their evening stroll, a young girl was heard to shout, 'Do me harder, you ginger tosser.' Then suddenly they noticed my bright red barnet. We got back to Blighty, and I was well and truly dumped.

MOTHER-IN-LAW MIX-UP
Randy bloke loses his way

After spending a long week on a course, I drove to my mother-in-law's house, where my wife was staying for the weekend. I had a huge pile of work to get through before Monday, so I figured if I could get most of it cracked that night, I could spend the rest of my weekend with my gorgeous wife. She and my mother-in-law headed off to bed at 1am, while I knuckled down to some hard graft. I finished at around 2.30 am and proceeded to get a shower, hoping to find my wife in bed in a state of semi-consciousness and ready for a spot of romance (a good hard shag) after a week apart. In nothing but my birthday suit, my mind and body raring to go and a semi lob-on rearing its perky head, I made my way into the main bedroom. Pulling back the quilt and whispering sweet nothings, I got the fright of my life when, to my horror, my mother-in-law screamed out loud. No-one had told me the room plans for that night. Needless to say, breakfast the next morning wasn't a pleasant experience.

FURNITURE FROLICS
Man disturbs tea run

One night my girlfriend and I decided to christen my mum's new sofa, while she was out on the town with a few friends. After the session I dropped the now full Durex into the nearest thing available – a used tea mug – and we settled down in front of the television.

Mum came home with a couple of her friends, and they sat in the kitchen to have a cup of tea and a chat. Needing some more cups, mum popped into the lounge and rounded up the few on the table, including the one that contained our little 'present', while we sat oblivious on the couch, engrossed in what was on the box. Exactly one boiled kettle later, we heard screaming from the kitchen, and what sounded remarkably like someone being sick.

DRUNKEN DISASTER
Man blows chance of shag

Last summer, I moved into a house with five mates: three blokes and two girls, one of whom I had a slight 'thing' for. My first night there, I got arseholed, hit the jackpot and retired with my extremely fit flatmate to her room. Nothing major happened, until I woke up to the sound of laughter. Noticing my mates, in stitches, at the door – and realizing the girl in bed had now risen – I deliriously asked what their problem was. Then I really woke up as I realized that my pants were around my ankles and I was squatting over the girl's laundry basket. As I caught the unpleasant smell, it dawned on me what I had done. Gutted, I looked at the girl and realized I'd never pull her again. I had been infamous for sleep-walking, but never for sleep-shitting. I hoped it was all a bad dream, until I looked in the basket to find the messy legacy on the girl's clothes.

GAMING SESSION
Heavy lover holes ceiling

One afternoon my girlfriend suggested that we play nude hide and seek in her bedroom. Her parents were somewhere in the house, but as I had only been seeing her for a couple of weeks I decided to chance it, stripped off, and counted to ten while she went and hid. Her bedroom was a small loft conversion and it didn't take a genius to figure that she was hiding behind the bed, but in my haste to reach her I jumped across the floor, forgot that the floorboards didn't quite stretch all the way across the eaves, and went straight through the living-room ceiling. Not only did my hairy arse interrupt her mum and dad's television viewing that afternoon, but they were also blessed with an unrivalled view of my swinging todger. I'm still with Claire, but they haven't spoken to me since.

MISTAKE WITH PANTS
Bragging leads to red face

After a busy evening clubbing, I found myself being taken home by a young divorcee for a night of passion. We paid off her baby-sitter and settled down to the evening's entertainment. Having to work the next day – and wanting to escape – I awoke early and left my conquest asleep. I noticed a pair of ski pants lying in a tangled mess with a pair of knickers inside them. I immediately retrieved the underwear as a trophy and stuffed them in my trouser pocket. I went straight to work and during my mid-morning tea break, I entertained my colleagues with tales of my previous night's exploits. I spared no detail and played to the crowd, building up to the finale: the unveiling of my lady friend's underwear. At the appropriate point, I whipped out the aforementioned smalls and proudly held them aloft. It was only when I saw my workmate's shocked faces that I lowered my arms to find not the scanty women's knickers I was expecting, but a tiny pair of slightly soiled cotton briefs. Last owner: my sexual partner's four-year-old daughter!

DISASTROUS LEAK
Novelty balloon

Believe me, safe sex can get messy. On the final leg of an infamous pub crawl I spotted a gorgeous redhead. Egged on by my mates, I decided to go over and chat her up. We got on great and the conversation and drinks flowed until closing time. By the time we left the pub, we couldn't keep our hands off each other. However, as Debbie lived with her parents and I lived with mine, we decided there was only one thing for it – we would have to have sex under the stars. So, I found myself on my back in a field, with Debbie riding me senseless. After the deed was done I had an urgent need to empty my, by now bursting, bladder. I staggered over to some trees and promptly began to relieve myself. I felt the customary warm sensation but realized that I couldn't hear the familiar sound of pee. I looked down and, in the moonlight, noticed I'd forgotten to remove the condom, which by now was inflated like a balloon with my piss. Before I could react, the weight of fluid pulled the condom off my cock, drenching my trousers and shoes in the process. Debbie, who had witnessed all this, was so impressed that she left me to stagger home on my own and completely avoided me in the future.

HORROR WITH PANTS
Tourist's toilet trauma

While on a business trip to France, I was invited to a party in a bar. Soon I got talking to a stunning girl, Francine. A shag seemed an absolute certainty, so I got fairly pissed. Suddenly I felt the need to have a crap, so I told Francine I'd be back. Spotting a sign saying 'Hommes', I made a mad dash and found myself in a dark alley behind the café with a door at the end. Inside was a typical French bog: two footplates and a septic hole in the ground. I dropped my kecks and laid cable, which proved to be pretty nasty. Then I realized that there was no paper. A sock just wasn't going to do the trick, so I decided to use my boxer shorts. Removing them required a real balancing act: I always had to keep one shoe on and not fall into the mire below. I couldn't leave the soiled boxers in the trap so I went out into the alley to find a bin. Just then, the far door opened, and Francine appeared. So I panicked and lobbed the boxers onto the roof of the khazi. She walked slowly towards me. I lit a cigarette. She came up, I leaned down to kiss her – and suddenly there was a rolling noise, then a splat next to my left shoe, as if a wet packet of sand had just fallen. It was my 'turd-ridden' boxers, which I had thrown onto a sloping roof. I spent the night alone.

ANIMALS & CHILDREN

PROPS POORLY CHOSEN
Cowboy attempts clean run

Back in the Sixties, the cult television show for us kids was *The Lone Ranger*. One of the lads, Barry, received the full outfit for his ninth birthday, and we were all immediately dispatched to find suitable props so that we could join his Lone Ranger gang. Mum had gone to the shops, so I searched through the house until I found some suitable material, and cut two holes in it to make a brilliant mask. Then we galloped off behind Lone Ranger to Dead-Man's Gulch (back of the Co-Op). As we passed through the throngs of shoppers however, I was suddenly whisked off my feet by my furious mother, who spanked me all the way home. Apparently, seeing her five-year-old son charging through the local shopping centre with her sanitary towel tied around his head had played a little on her nerves.

VITAMIN ALLOWANCE
Lovers provide refreshment

Shortly after the wife and I were married, she suggested that we try something new during our bedroom activities. Happy to oblige, I soon discovered that she enjoyed masturbating with various vegetables. One fine evening, after several drinks, we headed upstairs armed with a cucumber and embarked on a marathon session, during which the used cucumber ended up being discarded on the floor. When I awoke the next morning however, I let my eyes drift to where I had dropped the oblong vegetable and let out a loud scream. Sitting bolt upright, the wife followed my gaze and promptly followed suit. On the floor sat our two-year-old son, munching his way happily through the cucumber. Needless to say, that kind of sexual antic has only been repeated under the tightest of security.

PET TORTURE
A dog on heat

Visiting my parents for the weekend, I went into the lounge expecting to be pounced upon by my parents' dog, an adorable Yorkshire terrier named Crosby. But the dog remained prostrate on a blanket on the sofa, looking extremely sorry for himself. 'What's up with the dog?' I asked. My father burst out laughing and my mother put down the newspaper she was reading and stormed off, muttering, 'Oh don't start again, Harold!' Dad continued laughing hysterically, then explained: 'At breakfast, your mum decided to spray Crosby with flea spray. She got hold of him, laid him belly up and gave him a good old spray. But, as she was knelt in front of the gas fire, the flea spray ignited like in *Live And Let Die* and set the dog's balls aflame! Crosby sprang up and ran around with his balls on fire! I chased him around the lounge for 40 seconds before I managed to stop him and slap his balls to put the flames out!'

BROTHERLY LOVE
Cast-offs catastrophe

During his teenage years, my friend Pete did his fair share of wanking. Not wanting his mother to become suspicious about the rapidly diminishing supplies of toilet roll, he searched for alternative methods of 'absorption'. After dabbling with various materials – including a karate suit – he settled on an old pair of track suit bottoms, which he stored at the base of his wardrobe. The trackie bottoms served him well, until eventually he left for university, leaving them – and his past life – behind. But on returning for the Christmas holiday, Pete was met at the door by his 13-year-old sister, who appeared to be wearing a hauntingly familiar – not to mention rather rigid-looking – pair of track suit bottoms. Upon questioning, the innocent youngster replied: 'Mum's just given them to me.' Aghast that his little sister was unwittingly wearing his semen, Pete felt compelled to sneak into her room as she slept, steal back the track suit and wash clean the spunk-stained relic of his misspent youth.

UNFORTUNATELY MOCKED
Father adds insult to injury

While shopping in our local supermarket with my five-year-old son, Jordan, I noticed a young 'differently abled' girl walking through the fresh fruit section with the aid of a pair of tripod crutches. Jordan began staring, so I picked him up and we quickly disappeared off into the aisles. Having bought half the store, I paid for our groceries, then we joined the back of a large queue for lottery tickets. As we waited, the same girl walked past with her entire family in tow – prompting the ever-curious Jordan to tug at my trousers, point at her walking aids and demand, 'What are they for, dad?' Feeling myself going a deep shade of crimson, I gave the girl an embarrassed smile before saying to my lad, 'They're to help the girl walk better, son.' To my horror the girl looked me straight in the eye and bellowed, 'I'm not a girl, I'm a boy!' before storming out. Slowly. Needless to say, I didn't get to play the lottery that weekend.

UNPRINCIPLED SEAMAN
Man cheats to win bike

A couple of years ago, while on home leave from the Navy in my home town of Cockermouth, I was asked to take my little brother to the local Donkey Derby. On arrival we saw helium balloons floating in the breeze, and realized there was some sort of competition going on. We wandered off to find the relevant stand, and discovered that for 50p you could buy a ticket, leave your name and address, and attach half the ticket to the balloon. After a certain amount of time the ticket which had been sent back from the most distant place from the fair won a top-of-the-range mountain bike. I duly bought a balloon, filled in my details and let it go. My brother, however, simply wanted something to play around with, so I bought another one for 50p, pocketed the ticket stub and gave him the balloon. We enjoyed the rest of the day, and I thought no more about the incident until I went back to my ship in Portsmouth. On looking in my wallet, I found I still had the ticket from my brother's balloon. Our next port of call was the Canary Islands: I duly posted back the ticket and my brother received a nice new mountain bike, all courtesy of his dishonest older brother. To make matters worse, when next back home I sold the bike and went out on the piss for a couple of days on the proceeds.

CABLING INTERRUPTED
Dumper regrets unlocked door

The other Saturday morning the doorbell rang, and before I could stop him, my four-year-old son raced up and opened the door. 'Hello, young man, is your daddy home?' enquired the visiting lady. After a short pause for thought, my son nodded, took two steps back and opened the door to the downstairs toilet, where I was sitting on the bog. Fortunately, the door screened me from view of our visitor, but my son had perfect vision of the pair of us. Ignoring my wild, silent, imploring gestures to shut the door, he grandly announced that there was a lady at the door. I just remained silent, trying to maintain the pretence that I wasn't there and was simply a figment of his imagination. So, after staring at me for a good ten seconds, my darling boy turned back to the woman and duly informed her that, 'Daddy is having a poo.' Fortunately, this prompted the woman to mutter something about coming back later, before fleeing down the driveway. We never did discover her identity.

TRAINING TRAUMA
Daughter paints father
After a pretty horrendous training weekend with the Royal Marines
Reserves, I came home and fell asleep on the sofa – only to wake up to
a tingling sensation in my feet. My young daughter had taken my shoes
and socks off. I went back to my well-deserved kip. The next morning, I
found out what my daughter had done, but by then it was too late to do
anything about it. I just made a mental note to deal with her later. At the
camp, five minutes into a run with the lads and our instructor, I twisted
my ankle in a pothole and was carried off to sickbay. All gathered round
to see if it was a juicy injury (sick bastards, these marine types). Then
the doc took off my sock. To my – and everyone else's – horror, my toe
nails were painted with pink Barbie doll nail varnish! And did they believe
my story? Did they fuck!

PET CEMETERY
Shell holds hidden delight
My gran and grandad have kept the same tortoises since I was a child.
Because they are now fairly valuable, the duo are locked in a small hutch
every night and brought out again the following morning. My gran used
to do this, but last year she was in hospital for six months, leaving the
job to grandad. One afternoon I popped over for a beer, and while
the pair of us lounged in the garden, I asked after his pets. He said they
were fine, although 'Timmy' was so old now he didn't walk about much.
Bending down to stroke its head, I discovered that Timmy's shell was
nothing but a festering mulch of green rotting meat, infested with
maggots. The old fool had been putting his deceased chum in and
out of the hutch for months.

ADULT EDUCATION
Cousin gets eyeful
A few months ago my girlfriend had to babysit her young cousin. She
was told by the very conservative aunt that I was not allowed into the
house other than to pick her up at the end of the night. Needless to say,
as soon as they had gone I was round there – and with the little chap in

bed, was soon receiving outstanding oral sex on the sofa. I was in heaven, until I noticed her little cousin standing about a metre away, staring intently at my girlfriend's bobbing action. Leaping up, we fobbed him off with a story of 'that's what adults do'. All was fine until the following weekend, when my girlfriend got a call from her incensed aunt, who demanded to know why her six-year-old son kept trying to give himself a blow-job at the kitchen table.

DAMP FELINE
Pussy gets soaking

Some years ago I went to my cousin's engagement party in Greenwich, where the toilet was an outhouse in the back yard. When I needed to relieve myself, there was a long queue, so I decided to do it in the fish pond. In my haste I didn't realize that my aunt's cat was sitting at the water's edge, and the poor thing got covered. Shortly afterwards my aunt entered the garden and picked up the cat. While stroking it she said: 'The cat's all wet!' 'Oh,' I said, 'she must have fallen in the pond.'

THOUGHTLESS PRANK
Sprain causes night of terror

When I was at school, we used to play a game in our dinner break which involved locking some unsuspecting young lad in one of the lockers. The idea was that we'd roll the locker onto its side, kick it for a bit, then let the poor bugger out, who would usually stumble around dazed for a few minutes. One dinner break we locked someone in, rolled the locker over and gave it our customary kick, then couldn't unlock it. At first our prisoner thought we were joking, only realizing things were a little more serious when he heard the key snap in the lock. Dinner break ended and we still couldn't force open the locker, so I promised I'd return after school to let him out. But we had PE in the afternoon and I sprained my ankle playing football. Such was the pain, I caught the school bus straight home. It wasn't until later that evening that I remembered the locker, when my mum came off the phone saying, 'I've got Mrs Thompson on in a bit of a state,

wondering if you've seen her boy, as he didn't come home from school.'
I daren't own up at the time, but did get to school very early in the
morning, only to be confronted by the police, the caretaker – with
crow-bar – and the gasping boy.

DUMB CHILDHOOD ANTIC
Nipper sees stars

When I was a child, friends and I would play on the railway line just
outside our town. We would wave to drivers and passengers and
occasionally place an ear on the line to see if we could hear a train
approaching. One day I decided to listen, and squatted down, took hold
of the track and put my ear against it. There was a loud bang, a bright
flash and I landed, rather stunned, in a bush ten feet away. I'd forgotten
that there were three lines with one carrying the electric current.
Presumably my rubber-soled plimsolls and both hands making simultaneous
contact had saved my life. The short-term effects were some faint burns
down the inside of my arms and legs. Longer term was the mixture of
awe and derision with which I was treated by my peers. And of course
I never told my mother – she would have killed me.

APPALLING CHILD
Dad's pants sabotaged

When I was seven, my parents divorced and my sister and I went to live
with my mother and her new husband. My step-father ran the house like
a POW camp. According to him we were constantly 'disobedient' and as
punishment had to endure his incessant temper-tantrums, criticisms and
bullying. In reality we were average children and he was a complete
tyrant. My sister and I became increasingly resentful of him and spent
hours plotting his grisly death. One day he returned home from work
early with a 'mystery' illness and stayed in bed for two days. Of course,
he was unaware that we had smothered his Y-fronts with Deep Heat. He
never did have any more kids.

DEAD RABBIT CONFUSION
Your coney lives twice

We have a golden retriever who has a habit of digging up prized miniature rose bushes and making off with neighbouring dogs' bowls of food. Last weekend, he came in carrying the corpse of a very limp and dirty white rabbit in his jaws. One of our neighbours has pet white rabbits, so I freaked and called my wife to look at the damage. Fortunately there was no blood on the animal, so we decided to make it took like a natural death. We washed it and my wife blow-dried its white coat and brushed the fur. That night we placed the rabbit on Barry's lawn and sneaked back home for a fitful night's steep. Later in the week, I met my neighbour, who said: 'You know, a really weird thing happened to us last week. One of our pet rabbits died of old age, and we gave it a proper burial in the back yard. You won't believe this, but the next morning when we got up we found it on the back lawn all clean and white and bright!'

SHOW-OFF BOUNCED
Smitten child given shock

When I was eight years old I had a girlfriend called Antoinette. I thought we would last forever, until I saw her snogging a boy called Ross in the playground after school. I was gutted, but decided to try and win her back. My plan was to impress her with my football skills, so one afternoon I stood outside her house and began a lengthy session of 'keepy-ups'. Eventually she came to the window to watch, so I started getting a little cockier, and eventually lost control of the ball. She smiled, I waved, turned to get the ball, and got run over by a white Ford Sierra. All I remember is her scream as I bounced off the bonnet and somersaulted off down the street. I spent the entire Easter holiday in traction, and never spoke to her again.

WILD BEAST
Child finds unlikely toy

Not so long ago, I agreed to help my girlfriend babysit her nine-year-old niece at her sister's house, knowing a decent shag would be my reward.

Before long – with the brat safely tucked away – the couch became my jungle of love as I unveiled my surprise – a novelty elephant posing-pouch. With my glistening little chap fitting the trunk, and my sweaty balls swinging sweetly in its cheeks, I danced my arse off like a horny Zulu, all to the desired effect: the sopping jizz-filled pouch was finally abandoned and we embarked on a humping safari. In the morning, long after we had departed, my lover's sister gasped in horror as her daughter shook her awake and proudly said: 'Mummy, Look at my new mask.'

FELINE SURPRISE
Cat pierces love balloon

Last Christmas Eve, after a heavy week on the beers, I found myself in the company of a very attractive girl. Somehow I managed to convince her to invite me home, and despite our drunken state we found a condom and got down to business, before eventually nodding off. Sometime later I was woken by the sound of her alarm clock, and as she made no attempt to get up and turn it off, I jumped out of bed, and staggered around in the darkness until I found it. I then felt her cat jump up between my legs, and as the girl had woken up, I asked her to turn the lamp on. Glancing down, I then noticed that the condom I had been wearing was still attached to my knob. Worse, I had inadvertently managed to piss myself during the night, and the whole bulbous mass was swaying wildly between my legs. Then, as the pair of us stared in horror, the cat made a final leap and speared the balloon with its razor-sharp talons, covering the room in cold sperm and urine. I left so quickly, I never even found out her name.

BOLSHY BROTHERS
Drawing-pin drama

When young, it was not uncommon for my brother and I to engage in a bit of sibling fighting. One particular balmy night, we were too feisty to sleep. As my parents relaxed downstairs in front of the TV, I crept from my bedroom and into my brother's, where I set about knocking eight bells out of him with a pillow. The commotion led to shouts from downstairs for us to cease our rowdy fighting and get back to bed. However, a few minutes later, I was on the receiving end of an attack. This time my father bounded in, warning us that if he heard so much as another whisper, there would be trouble. He was a man who commanded respect, and we meekly returned to our beds. But there must have been mischief in the air that night, because I soon found myself creeping into my brother's room for one last belt – but he had scattered drawing pins across the threshold to his room! As I stole into the darkness, I miraculously avoided the many tacks that lay across my path, and set about pummelling the startled youth. His cries alerted my furious parents, and as my father's footsteps pounded the stairs I scurried out the room – incredibly missing the tacks again – just in time to witness dad's bare feet sinking into the drawing pins. You can imagine the rest.

UNHAPPY DISCOVERY
Balloon holds a surprise

When I was a young lad of eight or nine, my friends and I would use the recreation ground near where we lived as a shortcut to school. One morning my friend Dave and I climbed the fence and jumped down on the other side. As we got to our feet, Dave proudly held up a balloon which had been thrown away in the grass and proceeded to try to blow the thing up ready for school – a great talking point for nine-year-olds in any playground. As we walked through the rec, Dave struggled with the balloon, and he finally managed to get the thing going. It was then that I noticed a load of liquid in the expanding globe. As Dave attempted to get the balloon to full inflation, the liquid sloshed back into his mouth, where he swallowed it. He chucked the balloon down and said with disgust that the liquid had tasted 'salty'. It was only a few years later, when we were practising our new-found safe sex techniques with the local easy girls, that we realized Dave must have swallowed a mouthful of Harry Monk out of a used condom!

ROYAL SHAME
Child spoils the big day

It was 1981, and the country was gripped with Royal Wedding fever as Prince Charles and Lady Di got set to tie the knot. My parents, being staunch supporters of the royal family, decided to drag my younger brother and I down to Buckingham Palace so we could see the happy couple out on the balcony. Naturally, the nation's capital was heaving, and the throng around Buck House was awesome. Being an inquisitive ten-year-old, I wormed my way through the grown-ups' legs right to the very front of the crowd and stuck my head through the Palace railings – where it remained firmly wedged when I tried to pull it out. The next thing I knew I had a policeman on one leg, my dad on the other and my mum smearing margarine, kindly donated by a fat man from a hamburger stand, all over my ears. Nothing worked. Eventually a huge section of the crowd had to move out of the way so that a fire engine could get up to the fence. They had to cut a section out of the fence (which I wasn't allowed to keep as a souvenir) to free me, and the whole story made the papers. I not only ruined the day for my parents and a large section of the crowd, I was also responsible for an act of vandalism on the home of our great Queen. I apologize.

SPORTING SNACKS
Fat skier eats for two

When I was 10 years old I went on a primary school skiing trip to Austria. At the time I was a very fat and very short little boy, and my mum had elected to dress me in tight white polo neck jumpers, and emerald green, arse-hugging ski pants, which only served to emphasis my porcine features. Towards the end of an afternoon on the slopes, my mate Mark and I snuck off to a café, popped our skis on the rack, and headed inside. Mark asked me to get him a king-size chocolate bar while he went to the loo. I bought the food, but when Mark had failed to return after five minutes, I began to eye his share of the grub hungrily. Eventually I succumbed to temptation but just as I began to nibble at the top of the choccy feast, a group of Englishmen strolled in and stopped to stare at me. I can only assume they thought I was a local and couldn't speak English, as one nudged his mate and said, 'I bet that fat twat is going to eat the lot.' And I did.

KAMIKAZE FOWL
Quick meal

Having just moved into a three-bedroom bungalow, my wife and I
thought that it would be nice to buy our two small children a budgie.
The kids loved the idea, and chose a nice cage and toys, as well as a
chirpy little bird. Once back home, I hung the cage in the lounge and
while they stood underneath it, pointing and squealing, I helped the
wife with dinner. Eventually my son ran in, screaming that the budgie
had escaped. True enough, we found it flapping round the curtains, and
in the following excitement, it took refuge in the kitchen. Everyone then
had a hilarious ten minutes as the feathery sod thwarted all my efforts
to snare him with a tea towel. But the laughter came to an abrupt halt
when, for no real reason, the bird soared to maximum altitude, tucked
up its wings, and dive-bombed straight into the deep-pan chip fryer.
Yes, it did sizzle, yes the kids still have nightmares, and yes, for weeks
afterwards our mates would phone us, order Kentucky Fried Budgie,
then burst out laughing and hang up.

CHOKING DOG FIASCO
Golden boy gets rumbled

After six months of being blanked, I finally managed to secure a date with the girl of my dreams. We went first to see a film, then headed on to a top-notch restaurant for a meal. Things went much better than expected as Lucy became more and more amorous as the evening went on. I drove her home and she invited me in for coffee, but warned me that there would be no messing about, as her parents were in. Anyway, I sat down with her mum and dad and we all got along very well. So well, in fact, that I accepted her father's offer of a large whisky or two, which put me over the limit to drive. Even this wasn't a problem on my night of nights, as Lucy's old man kindly offered me the sofa to sleep on. Lucy and her folks went up to bed and I settled down, only to be nudged awake half an hour later by a giggling and slightly tipsy Lucy, who proceeded to treat me to the best shag of my life. When we were both exhausted but happy, Lucy snuck back up to bed and I fell asleep. In the morning, we all had a lovely breakfast and I reflected on my good fortune with Lucy's parents, who obviously had a lot of time for a pleasant, responsible chap such as me. Then, just as I was about to leave, their pet terrier came running in from the living room, choking and obviously in great distress. So, seizing the opportunity to win more brownie points with Lucy's folks, I picked up the mutt and performed a mini Heimlich manoeuvre. Lucy and I then watched in horror as a used condom shot from the dog's mouth and landed with a splat on the kitchen table, destroying my good work and banishing me from the house forever.

CANINE TREATS
Mother gives dog warm meal

The mutual dislike between myself and my girlfriend's mother stems from the fact that she hates animals, and her daughter has just moved in with me and my large black Labrador, Zac. In an attempt to improve the relationship between us, my girlfriend persuaded her to come round for dinner on the understanding that Zac would be locked outside. But somehow the bugger managed to find a way back in, and made his way straight for the daft bat, plonking his head on her lap in hope of some scraps. She reacted by frantically pushing his head away, which was followed by an audible 'phut' as she inadvertently popped a large abscess under his chin. A considerable amount of foul-smelling, slightly bloody pus shot out onto her expensive dress, leaving a great stain. She looked up at me, then opened her mouth and vomited all over the table, with Zac heartily lapping up whatever ran onto the floor.

HANGOVER HORROR
Fetch the retch rover

After getting violently pissed to celebrate my friend's birthday, he and I staggered back to his parents' house to crash out. I was directed to a room which was full of ladders and without lights, so getting to the bathroom was going to be difficult. As the room started spinning I decided that it would be best to puke on the floor and clean it up in the morning. According to plan, I awoke early but then reality reared its ugly head. A great spray of puke had gone over his mother's clothes and had liberally covered the bed. Have you ever tried removing dried vomit from the channels in corduroys? Keeping a cool head I scraped all the spew into a pillow case with a birthday card, deposited it in the neighbour's garden and put the sheets and clothes back in the washing machine. Later, while having breakfast with the family, an eerie scratching came from the door. It swung open to reveal their dog with a multicoloured pungent pillow case swinging from its mouth.

BALL GAMES
Teenage fiddling exposed

When I was 14, I would secretly masturbate in as many weird places as possible, and in secondary school it was not uncommon for me to tease one out during double history or a particularly dull maths class. Yet perhaps the strangest place of all was on the sports field during a games lesson. I was playing rugby on a cold November afternoon, and, becoming increasingly bored stuck out on the wing, I slipped my hands down my shorts to keep them warm. It was then that I decided to have a furtive jostle and proceeded to go at it hammer and tongs – climaxing in that inevitable warm feeling rising up my shaft. Suddenly someone shouted my name, and I looked up to see a high ball hurtling towards me. By now I had reached the point of no return, and, as the ball landed beside me and both teams stared, I gave an idiotic, buck-toothed grin ... and ejaculated into my shorts. I was never picked for rugby again.

WEIRD LOVE TRIANGLE
Faithful hound joins in

One night, feeling amorous, I convinced my girlfriend to don a figure-hugging basque and black fishnet stockings. She duly obliged and we soon got down to business. To get the best view of her perfectly-formed mesh-covered legs, I suggested we do it 'doggy fashion' over her favourite armchair. We were indulging in some frantic sex when I realized my right leg was too close to her two-bar electric fire. But I was too near the point of no return to change position, so instead I began to yelp involuntarily, which my girlfriend took as a signal of my increasing ecstasy. She started moaning and yelping in a similar fashion, and the sideways jerks I made to distance myself from the heat only made her more enthusiastic. Then I had an even stranger sensation. Just as I was about to come, her labrador stuck its cold, wet nose right up my arse. My body spasmed in every direction – with shock and pain – while my girlfriend was in ecstasy. I never told her about our third party!

HOLIDAY FIASCO
Cat-sitter lands in the shit

I was on holiday in Paris a couple of years ago, and was fortunate enough to have the loan of a friend's flat while he was away on business. The only thing he wanted in return for the flat was that I looked after his cat for the two weeks, which I agreed to do. Anyway, two days before my mate was due back, I decided to go out and celebrate my final 48 hours in Paris. I went on a bender with some friends, leaving a good supply of catfood and water for little Napoleon. When I came in from my epic binge, I could barely stand up. All I wanted to do was sleep, so I went straight to the bedroom and crashed out on the bed. Early the next morning, I woke up to the sound of a key in the lock, and looked up at my friend, who was looking at me in abject horror. The poor cat, having had twice as much as usual to eat, and nowhere to go for a crap as he hadn't been let out, had used the bed as a toilet, and I had spent an alcoholic night tossing and turning in his shit. It took a lot of explaining, laundry and several glasses of wine before my mate saw the funny side of things and believed I wasn't a shit fetishist.

BALLISTIC SHELL
Pet strewn over owners

Many years ago, my mother decided to buy two baby tortoises. As they were young, they didn't hibernate, and during the winter they were kept inside in a large plastic container, which contained some cabbage leaves and an electrically heated imitation rock. One Saturday morning, I popped round to visit, only to be told that one of the tortoises had died. After a brief inspection, however, I suspected that it could just be sleeping, and I managed to persuade the old dear to place it on the heated rock in the container and crank the power up in order to disturb it from its slumber. Five minutes of serious heat later, the tortoise gave a little shake, started emitting a strange hissing sound, and then exploded, covering us all in hot flesh and jagged shell.

LINKS HIGH JINKS
Golfer despatches bird of prey

I'm a keen golfer, and recently played a quick 18 holes one sunny afternoon. I was hitting the ball cleanly, and hard. At the fifth tee I selected my new driver with a 9.5 degree loft and larruped the ball down the fairway. It went low and hard and, to my horror, struck a passing kestrel, taking its wing clean off. It really was an horrific sight. The poor bird flapped around on the ground in a small circle, obviously in great pain. In an almost instinctive action I took a seven iron from my bag and put the raptor out of its misery. It was a quick, clean, humane kill, and I chucked the bird into the rough and continued my round – shooting a 75, which was below my handicap. But back at the clubhouse I was shocked to be hauled aside by two uniformed RSPCA inspectors. They had been told I'd been clubbing birds to death, and only when I explained that I had injured the bird first did they let me off – with a warning.

TIGHTS CONSUMED
Pet leaves painful reminder

While walking the dog one afternoon, my mum noticed that our mutt seemed to be having a little difficulty passing a strange-looking stool. On closer inspection, we both decided that it was in actual fact a small length of one of my mother's tights, and in a fit of generosity, she placed a firm foot on the piece of material that was dragging along the ground. My task was to then walk the dog along the road, thus pulling the offending article out of its arse. Neither of us realized that I would have to walk the dog for a good ten metres however, and when it finally popped out, the second leg headed back towards mum like a rocket, smacking her square in the mouth and giving her an impressive streak of shit right across her face.

COIN SWALLOWER
Child humiliates own parents

Fifteen years ago, as a wee seven-year-old, I decided it was time to find out what a ten pence piece would taste like. In full view of my parents, I stuck the coin in my mouth. My father yelled at me to spit it out at once. 'I can't,' I replied. 'I've swallowed it.' After my mother had got over her histrionics and rung round every doctor she could, she was finally assured that the best course of action was to leave the coin to pass naturally through my body. I was told that I had to shit in a bucket until the two shillings passed out of my arse. My poor parents had to wade through dozens of buckets of shit, morning, noon and night, searching for the elusive piece of silver. This went on for just over a week. I never had the heart to tell them that I hadn't really swallowed the coin, and planted it in the bucket when the joke began to wear thin.

STUDENT POLITICS
Steroidal bunnies set loose

While I was a student, I became mixed up in left-wing politics. Part of my initiation was to demonstrate my dedication to the protection of a group of animals which were being cruelly practised upon in the labs of the local university biology department. Some of the beasts really were being appallingly treated: skin was shaved from little puppies so that after shave could be tested; mice were force-fed with drugs; and rabbits were jacked up with steroids – all in the name of research. One night a gang of like-minded mini-revolutionaries and I decided to set free the rabbits – which happened to be the most accessible animals, as they were kept in hutches which backed onto the fields at the edge of town. We donned our balaclavas and black donkey jackets and crept down to the labs. Nobody was about, so we bolt-cropped the locks and opened the hatch doors onto the fields, and freedom. Naturally, we didn't stick around to watch the results of our handiwork. The following day at lectures we heard we had been successful: the rabbits had all got out. Unfortunately, we hadn't considered their steroidal history. It turns out that 35 rabbits made a grab for freedom – animals that weighed, on average, just over 25 lb each. Tragically, the rabbits had all been unnaturally thirsty due to steroid dehydration, and the first source of water they had come across was the cess-pipe of the local cereal factory. The poor bunnies had lapped at the fetid water until dead, and the local newspaper described the eerie scene the following morning as a 'floating, fluffy armada of death'.

RETRIEVER EXERCISED
Adult toy pleases Fido

Last year, after a heavy lunchtime drinking session, my girlfriend and I became proud owners of an 11-inch purple latex dildo which eventually ended up at the bottom of our wardrobe. This summer we went for a last minute holiday, and her dad kindly agreed to look after our one-year-old Labrador, Ralph, for the two weeks we were away. Everything went well, and we returned to find that the pair had become inseparable. Nothing was too much for the dog as far as Dad was concerned, and I felt jealous at the obvious bond that had grown between the two. You can only imagine my delight therefore, when on returning the dog one afternoon, the old boy nipped out to get Ralph's favourite toy. Yes, the silly twat had been round every park in the county with an amazing Dildo Retrieving Labrador, and was still none the wiser. Sadly, this triggered an outbreak of hostilities between my beloved and myself, as she's convinced that I put the toy in the basket on purpose. As I still have hopes of a reconciliation I would like this story to be attributed to someone with a different name from a different country.

BATH-TUB ACCIDENT
Younger brother receives marble

When I was a lot younger – just nine years old, to be exact – the Sunday evening rituals always included a weekly bath. My younger brother, Nigel, and I used to enjoy sharing a tub, and our mother would counsel us on the damage small objects could cause. Even though we had been warned, it didn't stop us sneaking model soldiers, bricks of Lego and countless other small objects into the bathroom to play with in the steaming water. One of our favourite bath-time toys was a large, purple, clear glass marble. One Sunday evening my brother and I were playing our soapy games, as usual, when a terrible accident occurred. My younger brother, having stood up to 'dive bomb' some of the floating plastic soldiers with pieces of Lego, sat down with a splash, having successfully taken out three men.

Nigel also sat down with a high-pitched scream, which drove me to have a fit of hysterical laughter, not knowing why he was causing such a fuss. The large purple marble, lurking unseen like a mine at the bottom of the soapy water, had been forced up my poor brother's brown star.

Consequently, poor Nigel spent a long, drawn-out evening face down on the kitchen table, having the glass marble removed with the aid of the ends of two teaspoons and a liberal amount of olive oil.

CRUEL DAD
Gullible child falls for dog-mess adage

When I was nine years old, as I was walking home from school one afternoon I had the misfortune to tread in a huge pile of dog shit. Engrossed at the time with ruffling through my collection of Topps Trading Cards, I failed to notice anything wrong at the time, and went on to walk the shit all through the hall, into the front room and out into the kitchen, leaving a trail of prints all over the house. My mum was really pissed off and scolded me harshly. But later on that evening I explained to my dad what had happened and he told me not to worry, because it was considered 'very good luck' to tread in dog shit. This cheered me up a lot.

So following my father's advice, the following day I trod in every pile of dog muck I could find. By the time I got to school I was covered in the stuff. Both my shoes were caked in shit, as were the bottoms of my trousers. I left a trail of faeces on the floor as I made my way happily into class – at which point my teacher went insane and sent me home to a battering from my mum. I obviously hadn't found any lucky excrement.

HELPFUL BROCHURE
Eagerness proves downfall

During my penultimate year of school, pupils were required to attend a careers seminar to help fashion a plan for our futures. Being an active chap, I decided to attend the lecture on the sports industry. Our speaker was a local entrepreneur who had formed a successful sports agency and, having been issued a copy of the company prospectus, I noticed that on the second page there was a picture of him with Colin Montgomerie, the rather rotund, red-faced Scottish golfer. Such a lucrative client must have proven invaluable to the company and, keen to make an impression, I saw it as an ideal point to bring up at the question and answer session. Right on cue, at the end of a somewhat tedious speech, I thrust my hand in the air and made my point to the speaker, who simply stared at me, totally bemused. 'See,' I began, holding the prospectus in the air for all to see. 'Colin Montgomerie.' Looking closely at the page, the entrepreneur made eye-contact and said, 'That, young man, is my wife and I.' Needless to say, my summer job at the company never materialized.

PARROT EXERCISED
Helpful child goes for a walk

When I was aged about ten my dad used to breed parrots. Not just ordinary parrots, but expensive and exotic ones he'd managed to get his hands on from somewhere overseas. Anyway, his job required him to be away a lot, and mum and I would took after the birds while he was gone. One time when he was away and mum was at the shops, I decided to be helpful and take his best bird for a walk – I figured it didn't get much exercise in the aviary. And I also thought I'd look pretty cool walking a giant parrot. I made a leash out of some string and tied it to the bird's foot, put it in a box and took it to the park. All during the journey it went crazy, flapping like mad, squawking and bashing into the lid, so when I got there I held the string tightly and immediately set the bird free. It flew straight up to the full extent of its leash, about three metres overhead – but didn't, as I had expected, stop and circle contentedly. In fact it scrammed so fast that the string tore its foot clean off, and it flew away screeching. All I was left with was a pathetic foot on a string. I looked for ages, but I couldn't find the bird. When dad got home I copped a clip over the ear and a month's grounding.

FLATULENT CAMEL
Beast causes ruckus

On holiday in Egypt, my mates and I realized that after a week hanging around the bars of Cairo, we should do the decent thing and visit the pyramids – and have a monkey about on the camels. We had a root around the ruins before paying one of the camel handlers a few pence and clambering aboard a bundle of bored-looking beasts. Almost immediately, my camel started farting – much to the amusement of my mates, and also a young American couple, whose porky little toddler found it especially hilarious. Predictably, the Egyptian camel owner went to town with the gag, pointing at me every time the mangy animal let rip, and sharing a smile with the Americans, who he was obviously tapping up for his next trip. For five long minutes, my mates and I were led around like idiots, the camel parping merrily away all the time. Just as I was getting off the beast, the American couple swaggered over and started haggling with the owner, when the camel opened its voluminous bowels straight onto the head of their over-fed child, spattering him with hard, lumpy shit. Suddenly, without warning, the kid's father lunged at me and gave me a hard thump on the arm, as if I was responsible, before joining his fretting wife, busy clearing poo from the mewling brat's face. Outraged but confused, all I could think of doing was picking up a turd and flinging it at the trio, which I did – before running off into a big crowd of tourists.

CHILD'S CLEAN-UP
Man's jacket holds surprise

A few years ago I was invited to my girlfriend's house for a first-time meeting with her young son. As luck would have it, the child turned out to be a likeable wee boy of four, who immediately decided that he wanted to be my friend. It wasn't long before his mum left to start preparing a meal. 'I'm Batman,' the little chap announced, eyeing up my denim jacket. 'But I haven't got a cape.' Determined to get into his good books, I whipped my jacket off and tied it around the little scamp's shoulders. Everything went well until, on his second circuit of the room, a condom fell out of the pocket. 'What's this?' squealed the nipper, excitedly. Panicking, I searched for an innocent – yet plausible – explanation. 'It's one of those tissues from the chicken and chip boxes,' I announced … then watched in disbelief as he exclaimed 'Just what I need!' and ripped it open. Unfortunately, as I made a lunge to grab the johnny, I caught the edge of the carpet with my biker boots and hit the deck with a massive thud. Concerned, my girlfriend popped her head around the door – just in time to see me spread-eagled across the floor while her precious son stood over me, frantically wiping his face with a strawberry-flavoured ribbed condom. I'm now banned from all house visits.

INJURIES ENDURED

SURFING HORROR
Drunk messes up foot

The Christmas before last I was in a pub being drunk and obnoxious, and was thrown out. Leaving the pub, I saw a huge tanker lorry driving very slowly up the narrow street, and thought I would have some fun. I jogged up behind the lorry and jumped onto the small ladder on the back, then got on the roof and tried a bit of 'urban surfing'. All was going well until the lorry suddenly sped up, and before I knew it I was lying on the roof as the thing pulled onto a dual carriageway. I went to the back of the lorry and climbed down the ladder, but the road was moving past very, very fast. Panicking, I decided I could jump off and simply manage to run along the road really quickly. The next few hours are a blur. Apparently a car ran over my foot, which was broken in six places, and I got a blood clot on my big toe. Besides this, I suffered bruising and contusions. Sadly, my toe went black and scummy. Three months later, when pulling on my jeans, I snagged the manky toe, and the whole bloody thing fell off. Thankfully, I can now walk again, but I don't do urban surfing anymore.

PATIENT MONITORED
Jostle ends in tears

Following a bad motorcycle accident last year, I awoke to find myself wired up in a bed in hospital, with, among other injuries, a broken right ankle. I had to suffer more than a week of bed baths and pissing into a tube before I was given use of a commode chair – a sort of potty on wheels I could use to move from my bed to the loo. For my first moment of privacy in ten days, I decided to check that no damage had been done to my little soldier, so I wheeled myself down to the toilets for a spot of well-deserved self-abuse. All was going well until, approaching the Grand

Finale, I stood up on my good leg and balanced myself against the basin. The chair then shot out from under me and slammed against the door, swinging it open and allowing the chair, me and my rapidly deflating manhood to fall with a crash into the bright lights of Ward 16. To cover my embarrassment I told the nurses I'd fainted – so they kept me in for another four days 'just in case'.

FLOUR FIASCO
Chef gets blocked

As any professional cook will tell you, long hours spent in front of the stoves can result in the condition we call Chef's Arse – where your ring becomes red-raw and sitting down is difficult, to say the least. The best remedy is a good handful of cornflour, up and around the offending area. I was halfway through a double-shift when Chef's Arse last struck. The chafing was unbearable, so, unable to locate the cornflour, I took a packet of plain flour into the loo, gratefully slathered it over my hairy arse, and finished my shift, pain-free. Next morning, I launched into my usual routine: black coffee, ciggy, followed by turd time – so I entered the loo, dropped my trousers and went for the big squeeze. My scream woke the entire house. My arse-spiders had meshed with the flour and sweat to create a near-impenetrable, hairy net over my crack, through which I'd attempted to crimp off a length.

DANGEROUS RUMPTY
Gigolo crocked by weak member

Out clubbing one night I noticed a girl smiling at me from across the bar. So I bought her a drink and ended up taking her outside for a quick knee-trembler. I was pounding away, with her spreadeagled over a parked mini, when all of a sudden the banjo string under my helmet snapped, and blood went everywhere, bringing a sudden end to the evening's entertainment. Sadly, five days later I was running out of excuses as to why I didn't want to have sex with my regular girlfriend, so I decided to blame her. With the lights off and teeth clenched, I slammed into her, and my knob nearly snapped in half. Blood gushed out, but amazingly she asked if I was alright, cleaned me up, and after a month of guilty cups of tea, and no sex, I'm back on the job again.

SPARKLER GOBBLED
Juggler regrets ring-toss

A few weekends ago, my mates and I had congregated for our usual Saturday afternoon piss-up when a girl we all knew arrived at the pub to show off her new £800 engagement ring. My friend Les asked for a better look, and as she proudly handed him the sparkler he tossed it into the air, deftly caught it in his mouth and 'hilariously' pretended to swallow it. Unfortunately, seconds later Les started to turn blue, followed by an enormous belch and the words, 'It's gone...' The poor lass then burst into tears and fled. It was three days and five craps before Les's wife was able to present the girl with her diamond ring, sparkling and as good as new. It was some small consolation that its passage had ripped a three-inch hole in his rectum, hospitalizing him for two days.

HOLIDAYMAKERS RELAX
Heat seeker loses body part

After finishing our exams, my mate and I took a well-earned holiday in Spain. After our first night out, we decided that the best way to cure our hangovers would be a long session in the hotel sauna. It was nice enough, with coals in the centre of the room and long, wide-slatted benches circling the wails. We were in there for about half-an-hour, and in his completely relaxed state, my mate's left testicle managed to fall down through the gap in the bench without him noticing. I eventually stood up to leave, and was halfway to the door when my eardrums were pierced with the most blood-curdling screams I have ever heard. My friend was lying on the floor with blood pumping out of his sack, and things didn't get any better at the hospital; I was left nursing a lone testicle in a surgical bowl, while the paramedics did their best to stop the bleeding.

VACATION INCIDENT
Youth clobbers lover

Last summer my mate and I went to Ibiza for our holidays, and one night, while having a game of pool, two amazing looking older ladies joined us and asked for a game of doubles. We played a few games, and then one leaned over and seductively whispered that she would like to give me a blow job that 'I would never forget'. I didn't need asking twice, and we headed straight upstairs while my mate took the other one away down the beach. Once in my room, she told me to lie down and strip and, true to her word, proceeded to give me some of the best oral sex I have ever had. As I approached the vinegar strokes I slipped my hands under the bedboard and moaned in ecstasy. Then, for some unknown reason, she slammed not one, but two fingers straight up my starfish. I sat up so quickly that I lifted the headboard clean out of its mounting, straight over my head and directly down onto her bobbing bonce. Not only did it knock her out, it also caused her to bite right into my bell end and leave a false nail up my arse.

HOLE PUNCHER
Man gets nuts in a twist

While working in a large furniture showroom, I was asked by the manager to lift a remarkably heavy worktop. Seeing me struggle, a workmate who shall remain nameless, and was working nearby drilling holes into doors – rushed over to help. Needing to use both hands, he popped the cordless drill into the waistband of his jeans, and leaned down to get a decent grip. As he did so, his belt pulled on the trigger, and the drill spun into action, promptly wrapping his scrotum round the 3-inch drill bit. We thought he was screaming loudly at that point, but when we were then forced to switch the thing into reverse to unwrap his squashed goolies, he very nearly burst our eardrums. When he finally returned to work, he had three stitches and a comedy John Wayne walk.

SNAGGED KNACKERS
Drunken show-off descends pole

Several years ago a friend of mine held her 19th birthday party at a local hockey club. A group of us decided to travel down from university in order to conduct a full weekend of drinking, which included imbibing several pints while watching the rugby on TV in the afternoon. We were all in high spirits before we headed off for the do, looking forward to a night of merriment. Plenty of drinks were had at the party and everyone had a good time. That is, until I went outside to clear my head. Once in the fresh air I was drawn to the hockey team's clubhouse, and in particular to the flagpole that stood next to it. I climbed onto the roof of the clubhouse and, when the party emptied out, leapt across to the pole and slid down, to grand applause. However, I had failed to notice a small cleat on the pole, which ripped a hole not only in my trousers but also in my scrotum – a wound that required 14 stitches at West Middlesex University Hospital.

SOFA SEX SHOCK
Lover loses old fella

My girlfriend and I had been together for four months when we decided, at last, to consummate our relationship. I'm not afraid to admit that I was nervous – I wanted our first time together to be special. In short, I wanted to prove that I was an insatiable sex god. We had the house to ourselves and began to get closer in the living room. Heavy petting, panting and foreplay ensued, and I pushed forward. But instead of getting that joyous, warm sensation, my willy was hit by a rough jolt which caused immense pain. On top of that, I was getting a strange feeling which can only be compared to a cocktail stick wiggling about in a bucket. After five minutes of very little pleasure and occasional agonizing stabs, I gave up and looked down, expecting to see my willy in tatters. Fortunately, I was still intact, but I found I had been shagging the gap between the cushions on the sofa. Instead of hitting her G-spot, I hit a metal spring and a copy of *Reader's Digest*.

REVELLER'S REWARD
The benefits of drunkenness

It was Hogmanay and I was out with my friends with one goal in mind: to get absolutely melted. We went from pub to club and became steadily more drunk. Next, after closing, we headed to a party where we drank vast amounts of Jack Daniels and vodka. We were thoroughly shit-faced. The next thing I knew, I woke up in hospital, in a bed and with a great urge to go to the bathroom. But I could hardly move. After several moments of investigation, I discovered that this was due to me being coated in tin foil. Having struggled, eventually, out of the turkey wrapping and staggered to the toilet, I returned to my bed to find a doctor waiting for me, ready to lecture me on the dangers of drinking. I'd been found by an ambulance crew at 4.45 am, two miles from the town centre, lying in a bank of snow. Apparently, I was lucky to be alive. The funny thing was, I found far more money in my trousers than I'd gone out with. I'd either robbed a charity box or been given change by people who had taken me for a homeless guy.

BLOODY SEX
Bellybutton agony

I was once having a relationship with a girl who decided to get her bellybutton pierced. I was all for this, and was even more up for it when I saw how sexy it made her stomach look. I was so turned on, in fact, that we got down to some heavy petting, which was going along swimmingly until she decided to pull my jeans down for some more hardcore action. Somehow, in the heat of the moment, the button on my jeans got caught up in her bellybutton ring. And as she tugged my jeans she ripped down hard on the ring. Blood squirted from her stomach

and she let out a howl. I quickly held a towel to the wound, hoping
it was just a slight scratch. But when we pulled back the bloodsoaked
towel we were horrified to find my girl's bellybutton, complete with ring,
hanging at the end of a strip of skin. Instead of spending the summer
with a beautifully exposed midriff my girlfriend ended up covering up
a stitched wound, which turned into a hideous scar.

SANDWICH HORROR
Hungry man gives love bite

My girlfriend and I had been going out together for a couple of months
when we decided we should go on holiday together. We thought a long
weekend near one of the Scottish lochs would be romantic, so we set off
in the car early one morning. A couple of hours into the journey, my
girlfriend reached into her bag and got out a French stick sandwich she
had prepared for the journey. As I was driving, I had no hands free, so
she held it to my mouth for me to take a bite. I bit into the sandwich,
which was ham, but felt something slightly hard between my teeth, so
clamped down a little harder to get through the piece of 'gristle'. Only
when I saw the look on my girlfriend's pale, shocked face, and looked
at the blood dripping onto my lap, did I realize that I had bitten
clean through to the bone in her finger. She later forgave me for the
incident, but was scarred forever.

DRAMA DOWN UNDER
Driver faces a hard time

Some years ago my tank squadron was engaged in training exercises in
the northern outback of Australia. We covered huge expanses of hot and
hostile territory with a driver nicknamed Horse. After one very long drive,
he stopped our truck, complaining that his face was burnt and he needed
a break. Remembering a choice purchase during our last visit to town, I
offered him a bowl filled with something that looked like Germolene to
soothe his burn. Horse smeared it liberally all over his face. Within
minutes, the poor bloke's head had ballooned up to twice its size,
sending him careering off into the outback, followed by a swarm of red
flying ants that were smitten by the smell of the freshly applied cream.

Everybody stood with their mouths open as I admitted that Horse was running around like an idiot with 'Sammy Stay Hard' erection cream all over his face. He hasn't retaliated yet, but after-sun on my cock wouldn't seem nearly as bad.

TOILET PREDICAMENT
Man trapped behind bowl

Twenty-six years ago, I fractured my femur and ended up in the North Staffs Royal Infirmary. After six weeks of bed-pans I was finally ready to take my first trip to the bog, for which I was to travel on a converted wheelchair with a hole that went conveniently over the loo. The nurse said, 'Press the button when you've finished,' and left me to perform. Unfortunately the button was behind me and, as I went to press it, the wheelchair tipped; I ended up arse over tit between wall and toilet. Try as I might, I couldn't get anywhere near that frigging button, so I lay shouting for help with my lungs fit to burst. Only after about 20 minutes did the nurse come to release me from my predicament. A few days later I shat the bed, and to this day I can't decide which was the most embarrassing incident of the two.

SKATE RINK LOVE TRAGEDY
How not to break the ice

As a hospital porter I was in lust with a nurse who bore a striking resemblance to Ali McGraw in *Love Story*. Fancying myself as a bit of a Ryan O'Neal, I reckoned the way to tempt her into my trousers was to recreate the film's ice rink scene. On the rink I murmured casually, 'Watch me go backwards'. Next thing I knew, I was lying in the hospital we worked at with two broken wrists. Urgent questions began to present themselves. How was I going to pull my trousers down? How could I piss? The answer arrived with Ali McGraw tangling with my trunks, though not quite how I'd intended!

GLASGOW KISS
Virgin blunders on first date

When he was 18, my friend Simon was still a virgin, so as a favour I arranged for my girlfriend's best friend to come out on a double date. Before the event, he was very nervous, and full of questions about who should make the first move, and so on. However, his date was bowled over by him and the evening was a great success – or it was until he tried to kiss her good night outside her house. You see, Simon had a problem with his eyes, which meant he couldn't judge depths properly (his dire performances on the football field proved this). As she puckered up, he leaned in for the kill, thinking she was about six inches further away than she actually was... and bang! He was travelling at a fair rate of knots when he head-butted her on the bridge of her nose, so she reeled back, stepped onto the rockery, lost her balance and travelled uncontrollably into her father's car. End result? One heavily bleeding nose, one broken wing mirror, and one short-sighted man still in possession of his cherry.

PAINFUL URINATION MISTAKE
Exploding radiator chaos

While touring the Lake District my friend drew my attention to the temperature gauge on my Fiesta, which was struggling to cope with the mountainous terrain. We pulled into the nearest lay-by and found the cooling system bone-dry. My friend began abusing and insulting the vehicle while I began searching for an appropriate receptacle in which to collect some water from a nearby brook. Realizing nothing was at hand, we decided to urinate into the expansion tank. I went first and the deed was completed without trauma. However, as my friend lined up his equipment with the filler cap a sudden surge of back pressure sent a hissing torrent of steam and boiling piss spewing from the orifice. My friend suffered no permanent damage, but to this day winces whenever he sees a Fiesta Popular.

WELSH ACCIDENT
River plunge horror

During my early teenage years, a bunch of mates and I would bike several miles to a river near Llangollen in north Wales. Here we had constructed a rope swing fairly high up on the bank, tied to the branch of a tree. We would swing out over the river and drop into the dark, still waters below – at times we must have reached a height of a good 20 ft before letting go of the rope. Anyway, the years rolled by, and in May this year we went back to the area for a few beers near our old haunt. The day was hot and dusty, so we decided to nip down to the rope for a dip. We staggered along the riverbank, and before long one of my mates spotted an old rope swinging in the breeze. He tore off his clothes and ran at the rope, getting a great swing out over the river, and let go a good 25 ft above the surface. To our horror, my mate splashed into just three feet of water and let out an horrific scream. It was the wrong place. He ended up with two broken ankles.

NIGHTMARE AT FESTIVAL
Mudslide ends in bloodshed

Like many people, I attended my first big music festival in my late teens. I was hoping to take shed loads of drugs and have as much sex as possible for three whole days. And I wasn't disappointed. The long weekend of debauchery was everything I could possibly have hoped for. I danced, drank and smoked myself into a frenzy, frolicked in the fields with topless hippie chicks and shared a sleeping bag with several of them. Basically, I managed to have the best time of my life. On the final Sunday I realized the one traditional bit of festival fun I'd not had yet was the mud bath. The weather had been too good, but I saw a way round this. Cunningly, I directed the water from a standpipe tap onto a path, and turned it into a perfect mudslide. People were cheering as I stood at the top of the path and prepared for my run-up. They clapped as I dived belly-first into the quagmire. But they were soon dumbstruck as I screamed like a pig halfway through my slide. Embedded in the track, and unseen to me, was a large piece of broken beer bottle. As I slid, it sliced into my stomach, leaving a seven-inch gash. I was rushed to hospital and had 16 stitches. I've never been to another festival since.

PYLON SHOCKER
Son hit by worried father

A lad I know works on the oil rigs, on a two-weeks-on, two-weeks-off rota, and whenever he's home he always calls in on his old Dad to see if any jobs need doing. On this one occasion, his Dad had asked him to weed the end of the garden, so, spade in hand, he set about the task. After a short while, he became aware of a small stone in his boot, which he struggled to dislodge. This proved more and more difficult as the stone worked its way further into his boot, so he leant on the leg of a nearby electricity pylon to try to shake it out. At this point, his Dad, who was washing up, glanced out of the kitchen window to see his son 'stuck' to the pylon, shaking his leg like crazy. Thinking the worst, the old man ran out of the house, picked up a spade and twatted his son with all his might in an attempt to break the 'current'. Instead, all he succeeded in breaking was his poor son's arm.

STYLING HORROR
Flash drink sparks disaster

While preparing for a lads' night out last year with five of my mates, I discovered one of them preening himself in the bathroom of my flat. Not wanting to get his hair sticky with gel or wax, my friend decided to use some of my girlfriend's hairspray. We took the piss out of him for a while, but after many beers forgot all about it. Later that night, my mate asked a girl to join him in drinking some flaming sambucas. However, due to the fact that he was less than coordinated after nine pints, he managed to spill the flaming liquid on his face. The mixture of fire and hairspray was disastrous, as his curly locks shot up. In the confusion the bloke next to him at the bar emptied a pint over his head; he succeeded in putting the flames out, but also covered a passing skinhead, who proceeded to punch the bloke and start a brawl. The only saving grace for my friend was that the blood he spilled covered up the burns on his face.

UNSAFE SEX
Condom instructions misread

When I was a lad I joined a Youth Training Scheme, and one week we were taken on an Outward Bound course in the Brecon Beacons. Once there we found, to our dismay, that the girls were split from the lads for our sleeping arrangements. Naturally, the next week was spent sneaking to and fro, and generally getting together at night was the prime concern of us all. But my mate Paul was very inexperienced with girls, and one evening he asked me about condoms. I told him to make sure he covered it all up because he didn't want the horror of crabs. Anyway, this one night we were all in the girls' dorm, quietly trying to have our shags, when a terrible piercing scream came from one of the beds. Out jumped Paul, who had a look of excruciating pain on his face: the stupid idiot had pulled the condom open and snapped it over not just his penis but also his scrotum. The tightened johnny not only caused awful pain in his nuts but also scooped a healthy bunch of pubic hair, causing agony to my naive friend.

FELLA CAUGHT
Fit show-off hurts pride

One Easter holiday, back at home from university, I decided to go down to my local gym. I'd been using the uni gym for a while, so thought it would be great to use the luxurious, private gym near my house. I picked up my mate, Richard, and we went down to begin our session. The first exercise we did was a shoulder and back work-out, which involved holding a 30 kg dumbbell in each hand. Then we'd shrug our shoulders back, holding the weights slightly apart and straight in front of us. Finally, we'd relax our shoulders and bring the weights back together in front of us. The first time we did this I nearly caught the front of my tracksuit bottoms, and thought, 'That was close.' Not as close as the second rep though: this time the momentum of the action caused the weights to clang together, catching my penis between the two metal ends of the dumbbell bars. The pain was, quite frankly, awesome. I dropped the weights, let out a high-pitched scream and fell over. Pulling down my trackies and skids, I saw a bloody pulp where my glans used to be.

FREAK INJURY
Good intentions cripple player

When I was studying in Ireland, I took up rugby. As my first season wore on, the lads and I were eventually scheduled to play a team which had quite a reputation for violent play. Considering that we weren't the most talented outfit to have ever taken the field, we decided to accept the challenge with a 'do or die' attitude, hoping things would eventually swing our way. They didn't, and to make matters worse our star player, Alan, dislocated his hip after a particularly ferocious tackle. He was clearly in a lot of pain, so we all stood back to watch the medic who, in one swift movement, managed to slot the hip back into its socket. Then Alan began a long, blood-curdling scream. To our horror, we realized that one of his testicles had also been jammed into the socket, and was now firmly held in place by the hip. Incidentally, Alan managed to rip a vocal chord with his screaming.

COSMETICS INSERTED
Adventurous lover pays price

A few weeks ago, in preparation for a romantic restaurant meal, my girlfriend decided to manicure her nails, even going to the extent of adding a few false ones. The meal was a success, and afterwards we headed home for some serious bedroom activity. In a frenzy of drunken foreplay I decided to stick an adventurous couple of fingers up her arse, and she immediately returned the favour. This lasted for a few minutes until her arm started to feel a little tired, so we knocked the fingering on the head and got down to business. Everything was fine until the following morning, when, during my morning visit to the toilet, I experienced a feeling of some discomfort. Assuming that my girlfriend had probably stretched my rectum with her enthusiastic finger-thrusting, I didn't panic; but after a few agonizing days I finally came to the conclusion that there was some serious damage up there, and reluctantly booked a trip to the doctor. It was then that I had the worst shit of my life – it felt like a herd of hedgehogs were passing through me. Afterwards, to my amazement, there was a bright red fingernail sitting in the bowl. Still, it saved me an expensive removal operation.

CHOPPING HORROR
Engineer leaves lover with small tip

A few years ago I was working on a YTS engineering course and I had a nasty accident, chopping the end off my right index finger with a milling machine. I was rushed to hospital where, luckily, they managed to sew my severed finger back on again. After several weeks, my bandages were removed and I was horrified to find the finger hadn't healed properly, and was still very scabby. It was a nasty sight, but the nurse assured me this was quite normal, and all would be well within a few weeks. Anyway, two weeks later I was indulging in some vigorous 'finger sex' with my girlfriend after the annual Judo Club Disco. When I'd finished pleasuring the lucky girl I was horrified to find that the end of my finger was missing! After a vigorous body search we eventually found the offending stub, and I'm happy to say my fingers are now all in one piece.

PLUMS IMPALED
Innocent game ends in agony
When I was about 16, a mate and I were up to no good in one of our local parks on a Sunday afternoon. As it was getting a bit late, we decided to jog through the park and catch the bus home, pausing only to play a game of 'leapfrog' over some rusty metal fenceposts. My mate found the going hard as he was only 5 ft 3 in, and he eventually gave up in order to watch me hurl my 6 ft frame over the posts. Sadly, as I gained momentum and attempted to hurdle the seventh – and last – post, my foot twisted in a divot. Unable to stop, I soared through the air, impaling my bollocks on the razor-sharp rusty tip and coming to an immediate halt with my feet hanging approximately six inches off the ground. Climbing off in agony, I discovered an inch-wide gash in my sack, with what looked like a white ball protruding from it. When my mother saw the damage, however, she just laughed, cleaned my wound and told me it would heal within few weeks. To cap it all, my pubic hairs grew into the cut as it healed, forcing me to split the new flesh as I pulled the little buggers out of my pustulous 'nad.

INMATE EXAMINED
Student rips lining
While working as a medical student one hungover Monday morning, the consultant asked me to examine a patient. All would have been well, had the patient not been a huge prisoner with a severe case of rectal bleeding. To ensure he didn't escape, he was attached to a guard via a six-foot chain that went under the door. I donned the glove, and inserted my finger up to the knuckle. I then twisted my digit to examine the prostate gland, but in my still-drunken state gave it too much welly, and my fingernail ripped through the glove and sliced into his tender fudge pipe. Screaming with rage he leapt forward – ripping his arse more – followed by a thump and another scream as the guard was pulled off his seat and into the door.

IRONING BOARD MISHAP
Paralytic man gets interesting scar

One afternoon, a friend had a few problems that required discussion over a few pints in the local pub. One thing led to another and before I realized the time, my friend and I had sunk one too many and staggered home. I was living in student accommodation at the time so the house was in a right state – shite everywhere – including the ironing board and iron just outside my room. Expecting my girlfriend to pick me up in an hour or so, I headed off to iron a shirt, but a tremendous fatigue entered my body and I thought, 'Well OK, just a quick lie down'. Six hours later I was woken by the telephone ringing. I crashed out of my room, knowing I was horribly late, at exactly the same time as one of my house mates picked up the phone and shouted to me that it was my girlfriend. To this day, I cannot explain or comprehend why I did what I did, but, on hearing my mate, I grabbed the iron thinking it was the telephone and felt it sizzle my cheek as I held it up to my ear. It had been on for six hours and by this stage it compared to the heat generated at the core of the earth. I looked in the mirror and saw V shaped indentations burnt onto my cheek. You could even see the holes where the steam comes out. The public humiliation lasted almost as long as the scar.

STICKY WICKET
Squaddie sticks to metal

While serving in the Royal Marines in Norway, my company was stationed in an isolated hotel, 60 miles from the nearest town. For entertainment, Saturday night usually consisted of a meal and lots of beer, followed by a an excursion into the cold air to have a piss. On one such night, one of the lads staggered out, had a slash, gave his little fella a shake, and turned to head back to the hotel. Unluckily, he walked straight into a metal dustbin before he had zipped up, and naturally his dick stuck fast to the minus 20 degrees metal. Ten minutes passed before we realized he hadn't returned and we dashed outside to find him walking backwards, pulling the bin along as if it was his lost friend. He thawed out at the hospital and returned two days later with a big bandage round his todger.

BROTHER AIDS RECOVERY
Sibling's lethal fingers

A couple of days ago my brother was rushed to hospital with appendicitis, and underwent an emergency operation. Feeling slightly guilty that I hadn't realized the seriousness of the situation when he first complained of a sore abdomen, I walked to the hospital determined to cheer him up. When I got there he seemed rather depressed – he'd only been out of theatre for a few hours – so to raise a smile I leant over and gave his foot a brotherly tickle. He jumped, and gave a contented chuckle, and then blood started streaming through his robe. The movement had ripped out all the stitches, causing his stomach to split open and pump its contents onto the bed. Naturally, I didn't speak to him again until he was safely out of hospital.

WIPE LAST STRAW
Player suffers post-match pains

A few years ago, while playing in an office five-aside game, I took a heavy knock which threw me against the goal post, damaging my right shoulder. The pain was unbearable, but although I whimpered off the park, I couldn't bring myself to cancel a dinner date with my girlfriend and her parents, who I was meeting for the first time. Dosed up on heavy duty painkillers, I went round to eat. Dinner went very well, and despite the occasional grimace, nobody seemed to notice my agony. After dessert, and some well-received double whiskeys, I stopped off at the toilet before heading home. As I reached round to wipe my arse however, I heard a sickening crack as my shoulder completely dislocated itself from the socket, leaving my trembling arm locked in full wipe position. Which is exactly how my girlfriend found me after I passed out, mid-scream.

BATTERIES INCLUDED
Couch potato feels the heat

One Christmas, about seven years ago, I was lying in bed in my parents' house watching TV. When I tried to change channel, I discovered that the remote wasn't working, and despite whacking it on the bedside table, it refused to come to life. It was bloody cold, so I took the batteries out and popped them under the pillow to warm some life into them. Five minutes later, still nothing, so I put them in the warmest place I knew – right between my buttocks. Then I realized that the batteries were leaking – the pain was incredible, and I ran to the bathroom. Keeping one leg on the floor, I lifted the other up into the sink, and furiously splashed water onto my burning starfish. It was then I realized I wasn't alone. My father had been woken by my groans, and was standing behind me with an extremely stern expression. Eventually he accepted my explanation, but he rarely lets me near the remote when I'm at home now.

MORNING SHAVING INCIDENT
The man who licked his razor

One morning, after staggering bleary-eyed from the shower, a glance in the mirror confirmed I needed a shave. As I had little faith in my hand-to-eye coordination so early on in the day, a wet shave was out of the question. I grabbed the electric shaver and switched it on. I don't remember which thoughts had crept into my semi-conscious mind, but they certainly had nothing to do with the job in hand. I stood looking at the razor, feeling its vibrations in my hand and listening to the hypnotic hum. Then I inexplicably brought it slowly towards my face and licked it. I stood motionless, transfixed by pain and mesmerized by my sheer stupidity, watching droplets of deep red blood rapidly appear and spread from the tiny grazes across the tip of my tongue. The bathroom mirror misted up once more. I was late for work.

WHEEZING IGNORED
Asthmatic suffers for threat

When I was at boarding school we slept in dorms. One night, I awoke to the sound of ferocious movement of sheets and heavy panting to my right. Knowing that the lad in that bed was an asthmatic, I went over to check that he was okay – only to find him secreted with a torch under his sheets, having the tug of his life. When he heard me chuckling, he emerged from his tent of sin and said that he would kick the crap out of me if I were to ever mention the incident. He was a big fella so I kept my mouth shut, and when I heard the same sounds a couple of nights later I turned over and tried to go back to sleep. Five minutes later, there was a thud, and I was greeted by the sight of the big man rolling on the ground, turning purple. He ended up in the medical centre, while I had a great night's kip.

THICK FOG
Care worker hospitalizes wards

Working as a care assistant, I was recently 'volunteered' to supervise a group of unruly kids on a canal barge trip. I soon understood why my work colleagues were so keen to stay in the office: four hours of navigating around dead dogs and shopping trolleys while attempting to control a load of screaming, hyperactive children. But suddenly, near the halfway mark, we hit a stretch of the canal blanketed by thick, odd, yellowish fog, apparently emanating from a house on the bank. There was nothing else for it: inspired by boredom and exasperation, I grabbed the set of bongos I kept below deck and sat cross-legged on the bow. As the barge drifted into the sepia gloom, I began to strike a tribal beat – and, grinning wildly, the kids began to dance. It was like something out of *Apocalypse Now*. We were still chuckling, in fact, when we got home. And then we were told there'd been a fire at a local chemical refinery, and one of the tanks had leaked toxic, sulphurous fumes across the area. With the noise of the engine, we hadn't heard local radio reports cautioning people to stay indoors. Three of the children had to spend the night in casualty before getting the all-clear, and I was promptly fired.

COCK BEHEADED
Man suffers friction burn

Two weeks ago I was sitting watching TV with my girlfriend, when I decided the afternoon could be better spent performing lewd sexual acts. Leaning across to kiss her, I moved my hands down to her trousers and undid the first button, only to be stopped dead in my tracks and sweetly told that this was one of her 'special' days in the month. Determined to extract some gratification from the moment and noticing that her tight trousers were made of Spandex, I decided some mutual rubbing may be in order, and placed my penis between her legs. The subsequent frottage quickly reached a frantic pace, but as I embarked on my vinegar strokes there was a very quiet 'ping', followed by an agonizing rip. Looking down, I was confronted by horror. My foreskin had been ripped off entirely, exposing a huge blue vein that was spraying blood everywhere. On arrival at the local hospital, a nurse gingerly held my pecker for examination – and I immediately grew another stonker, requiring a further two agonizing stitches. I'm now fully prepared to become a monk.

DRUNKEN EXPLOITS

COPPER CAUGHT SHORT
Plod showers unfortunate corpse

I'm a police officer, and a few years ago I was out on night patrol with my shift partner, Dave. The sarge radioed us and explained that there had been a death at a nearby top-floor flat, and that he would meet us there. When we arrived we found an old dear, completely dead, with her head resting on the toilet seat – tragically, she had passed away while attempting to vomit. I went into the living room and began filling out the forms, when the sarge suddenly got another call, and shot off, taking Dave with him. Ten minutes later I had finished the forms, and now had a more pressing problem – I was desperate for a pee, and couldn't use her sink as it was full of washing. I lasted about an hour-and-a-half before I could take no more. Straddling the old woman, I let rip; using all my skill to keep the golden stream about three inches from her wrinkled face. At that moment the sarge walked in, followed by Dave, two undertakers and the woman's middle-aged daughter. To round things off, I zipped up so quickly that the daughter saw me splash warm piss dribble all over her dead mother's head.

ROUNDABOUT DROP-OFF
Drunk disembarks at wrong stop

Some time back, on returning from a trip to America, I collected my BMW from the car park, and started the drive back home. In an attempt to avoid the motorway traffic, I decided to stick to the back roads. Then, as I pulled up at a mini roundabout, I was stunned to see a man lying in the middle of it, bleeding profusely and unable to speak. I called an ambulance, but five minutes later, a car came screeching to a halt next to us. A bloke leapt out and said, 'Oh thank God, there he is.' Apparently, the victim had also arrived on a flight, but had cleared customs so drunk he could hardly walk. In an attempt to get him home without puking, his mate had put him on the back seat, where he'd chosen to sit with his head hanging out the window to get a bit of air. As they hit the roundabout, the door had swung open, sending the fool flying into the road. The driver had gone on for five minutes before he had realized what had happened. Amazingly, the drunk recovered during this story, decided to headbutt his friend and a fight started in the lay-by. They didn't even notice me leave.

STUDENT SCORCHED
Scally dabbles with fire

During my final year at university I lived in a student house with a Scouser and other assorted drunken yobs, where we had a tradition: whoever lasted longest on the piss would set off the smoke alarm on their return home. So it came as no surprise at 3 am one morning to be woken by an alarm. Placing a pillow over my head, I waited for the triumphant drinker to reset the alarm and head off for bed. However, after ten minutes it became obvious that something was different, as a girl's screams penetrated the electronic wail. I tumbled out of my pit and followed the screams to the Scouser's room, where I was greeted by the sight of his bird jumping up and down on the bed, half naked, waving a sheet at the smoke alarm – while the Scally ran about with his dressing gown on fire. It turned out that when his girlfriend had spurned his offer of a night of lurve, he'd waited till she was asleep then, bored, started lighting his own farts – until he produced such a ripper that he set his nightwear on fire. After extinguishing the flames, we of course called him Ring of Fire for the rest of his university life – a fact I shall remind him of when I attend his wedding this summer.

GENT'S CONFUSION
Stag night toilet horror

It was my stag night and I was out with a bunch of mates. We followed our old pub crawl route and were about halfway down the card when, several pints and a gallon of Nelson's blood later, the call of the porcelain was sounded. The pub we were in had been refurbished so I made enquiries and staggered, head down, in the direction of the bog. It took forever to fight my way through the crowd but, finally, I reached the white door I had been seeking. My back teeth were floating, so I cared little for decorum. Therefore, I unzipped as I opened the door, and had myself in hand ready for immediate release. Pissed and bladder driven, I crashed through the white door to find myself faced by another. I blundered through this second door and, in my head-down position, marvelled at the extent of the refurbishment. There was carpet, loud music, flashing lights ... and atmosphere. I raised my head to locate the shiny white bowl, only to find myself, dick in hand, confronted by a roomful of gaping revellers frozen by the shock of what they saw. Not to mention two large bouncers heading in my direction. Mustering all the dignity I could, I glanced round the room, shouting back through the door, 'No, he's not in here!' I retreated and vacated the pub, gathering the lads as I went. We bundled out of the boozer, giggling and farting as we went, with me pissing at the same time – and with the angry shouts of the bouncers ringing in my ears. At this point, my prospective father-in-law – having been stupid enough to accompany me in the first place – made his excuses and went home, after leaving me in no doubt as to what would happen if I failed to make it to the wedding ceremony on time. Fortunately, I did.

KARATE COCK-UP
Macho man's shortcomings

In the middle of an all-day drinking binge with a friend of mine – who happened to be a karate instructor – we decided to pay a visit to a house where several of our friends lived, to stretch the day's fun as far as possible. Then all of us went into town to a pub, where, with the usual brash bravado, play-fights started to develop. My friend, who was very much the worse for wear, then decided to challenge everyone to a karate battle. Naturally, everybody declined, which led to the drunken martial arts instructor becoming more and more agitated. He loudly proclaimed that he could whip anyone with just his little finger, which was met with howls of derision. He next shouted that he could beat everyone with his ear, his eye and, finally, with his cock. When this final bullshit claim produced no takers, he unzipped his jeans, pulled out his flaccid johnson and began waving it in the air shouting, 'I could have you with this!' What he hadn't noticed was that the window – which made up one side of the pub – had filled with dozens of curious on-lookers, all of whom were loudly applauding his humiliating performance. To this day, he's still known in town as 'Maggot'.

LAVATORIAL MÊLÉE
Drunk man imagines assault

A few months ago a friend and I went on a real bender. Nothing extraordinary about that, you might think, except that we live in a part of London with less nightlife than a Norfolk village, and it was already 10.30 pm. However, we decided to try an illicit drinking den in our manor which was, reportedly, open all night. Amazingly, we got in, and proceeded to neck premium-strength imported lager at speed. After a few hours a bloke sat in my chair as I was buying a round. I asked him to move, but he ignored me and when my mate went to the bog I simply sat in his vacant chair. A few seconds later the ignorant man got up and followed my friend to the toilet, so I followed to check nothing untoward was happening. As I swung open the bog door I saw my mate holding his nose, and sprinted to get the huge bouncer on the door. He steamed into the toilet, dragged the man out and kicked the living shit out of him, before turfing him out into the night. Only later did my friend tell me that all he was doing was blowing his nose, while the poor chap who took a leathering calmly had a slash.

FILTHY COCKTAIL
Wounded man's sick drink

At a college party several months ago, I found myself in the kitchen, drunk, and messing about with a knife. My friend and I were taking turns spinning the knife in the air and trying to catch it by its handle as it came down. Naturally, after several drunken attempts I missed the handle and grabbed the knife by the blade, causing a really deep gash in my finger. In our pissed state, my friend and I deemed the wound not serious enough for a trip to the hospital, and decided to drain my blood into a glass before attending to the wound. We did this successfully, managing to get about a third of a glassful of blood, which we topped up with vodka, Worcestershire Sauce and a few drops of Tabasco. We gave the drink a swirl, and decided to present it to the next person to walk into the kitchen. I would just like to take this opportunity to say to my mate Laney: that's the most authentic Bloody Mary you'll ever have.

MANMADE COCKTAIL
Jilted lover gets dousing

Having been recently dumped by my girlfriend, my mates decided that I needed cheering up and dragged me down the local nightclub. I was having a brilliant time, when the ex suddenly walked in with her new boyfriend in tow. Spotting me, the pair performed a victory snog right in front of me, before heading for the bar. Determined to dish out a suitable punishment, I nipped to the toilet where, with the help of several revellers, I filled a pint glass with warm pee, and headed out to the bar where they were standing. My plan was to launch the pint over my shoulder catching them square in the face with piss, but as my arm shot up, I noticed that they were watching my every move. Panicking, I tried to stop my arm, but succeeded only in pouring the frothy liquid straight over my head and down my back. They laughed so much, one of the bouncers brought over some chairs, shortly before throwing me out.

DRUNKEN HIGH JINKS
Vandal caught out by cone

Walking home after an evening of heavy drinking several years ago, a couple of friends and I decided, irresponsibly and in typical sad 15-year-old style, to do a spot of vandalism to liven up our dull journey through the rain. On the first quiet street we walked down we pulled up several 'For Sale' signs, and used them for spot of improvized 'street jousting'. This was followed on the next street by 'hedge diving', and in the third street we played 'steal the bike saddle'. On the fourth street we came to we were pleased to see that a row of traffic cones had been lined up around a workman's hole, obviously positioned there for three drunk gits to kick into the street for a game of football. We walked along, taking turns to thwack the cones as far as we could. At the last cone, I decided to really go for glory, and took a long run up before aiming a vicious Lorimer of a kick at a Ford Escort that was parked right in front of me. Tragically, the workmen had obviously planned ahead. They'd placed the last cone over a concrete bollard, and I subsequently spent six weeks in plaster with three broken bones in my foot.

BARFING BLUNDER
Party-goer shames girlfriend

My girlfriend and I arrived late at her boss's house party so, to make up for lost drinking time, I started to gulp down the free-flowing wine. Suddenly, I felt very ill and rushed to the bathroom. On arrival, I couldn't find the light. As I was in a desperate hurry, instead of feeling for the loo, I headed for a chink of light which turned out to be the window, and just managed to get my head out in time. When my eyes cleared, I realized that below me was the glass roof of the conservatory where the party was going on. I went cold when I saw the puke sliding slowly down the roof and the sea of appalled faces – including my girlfriend's boss – staring up at me through the glass.

BURSTING BLADDER
Party treats get a hosing

Arriving late for a party after a few drinks in the pub I charged upstairs to the toilet, only to find it engaged. Luckily it was one of those houses in which the bath was in one room and the loo in another. Desperate and bursting, I figured I would simply piss in the tub, so I lunged for the bathroom. After 30 seconds spent fishing unsuccessfully for the string light-pull, I shuffled into the near blackness, bumped into the bath and gratefully let rip. One hour later, the hostess mentioned to me that the dozen mini-trifles, two jellies and the gateau we'd just eaten had spent the earlier part of the evening defrosting – in the bath.

FATAL ATTRACTION
Stray punch floors pest

Unwanted attention is frustrating at the best of times, but during the three years of your life when you're supposed to be nobbing yourself lame, it's positively infuriating. At university I was unlucky enough to attract the attention of the most irritating girl on campus. She was fat, noisy, always stuck her nose in where it didn't belong, and followed me around with a look of puppy dog adoration on her face no matter how often I told her to go away. After several months of this style cramping I'd had enough, and I told anyone who cared to listen that I was sick of her and I was going to put a stop to her evil ways. One night in the bar I was drunkenly ranting to some friends about what a cow she was when, unseen to me, she sat down just behind me. I had become highly animated by this point and told everyone that I would like to knock her out. I illustrated this by swinging a giant haymaker. Unfortunately, I swung right round and lamped the girl in the face, knocking her clean out of her seat, and splattering her face with blood. Everybody assumed I'd done it deliberately and for months I was labelled as a woman-beater, while she became very popular as the innocent victim.

PUBLIC ORATION
Wedding comes to abrupt halt

During the summer of 2000, I had the good fortune to be invited to a friend's wedding in the north-west of England. The best man has always been known to like a drink, but we were somewhat surprised at how quickly he succeeded in getting pissed on the day itself. The reason, he explained in a drunken slur, was that he had forgotten his speech, and was suffering a sudden bout of nerves. But he seemed to have pulled himself together by the time the reception started, and when the groom's polite thanks came to a close, everyone was ready for a few entertaining stories from the best man. Standing up, he slowly unzipped his trousers, pulled out his manhood, and announced to the stunned crowd, which naturally included several elderly relatives, 'I have a massive cock.' Then he sat down and clapped like a rabid baboon. Incidentally, he has never been seen since.

REVELLER REPULSED
Greenie finds new home

During the Christmas party season in London, every late-night tube home is packed with drunks – which is how I found myself opposite a smartly dressed middle-aged woman who must have had one too many and fallen asleep. Sitting beside her was a scruffy old wino who was drifting in and out of consciousness and swaying all over the place, finally slumping with his head inches above the woman's arm. A stream of green, lumpy mucus then began to stream out of the old lush's mouth, falling into a neat pile on the woman's arm, until the train bumped into a station and the old man slumped in the other direction. The woman jerked awake, and as her eyes opened she caught sight of the green slime on her sleeve. Before my astonished eyes, assuming it was her own, she greedily gobbled up the old man's mucus.

SAD TOILET EPISODE
Man confuses genitalia

I was standing in the lavatory during a rugby international at
Twickenham, when in lurched a smartly dressed but obviously drunk
middle-aged chap. On reaching the latrine, he unzipped his fly and pulled
out what he thought was his penis and began to pee. Unfortunately it
was his testicle he had in his hand and consequently a large stain
appeared down his leg along with a growing pool of urine around his
shoe. Oblivious to everything, he finished, shook off his testicle, zipped
up his fly and wandered out.

HI-FI INCONTINENCE ERROR
Drunken party confusion

I was sharing a house with three friends and we had decided to throw
the customary house warming party. The usual preparations were made –
turning the TV to face the wall, putting up little direction signs to the
toilet, filling the fridge with thirty quid's worth of lager etc. However, a
party would not be much of a party without music, and so my flatmate
Justine's Panasonic ME 109 turbo bastard midi-system was brought out
into the living room.

    As parties went, this was a bloody good one. At about 3 am, my
eyelids grew heavy with lager and I nodded off on the settee. Sometime
the next morning, I was rudely awoken by Justine, who was very pissed
off, and subjected me to a barrage of foul-mouthed insults. What the hell
had I done? Justine pointed to her pride and joy, the Panasonic. 'Lift up
the lid,' she demanded. I did as I was told, then immediately wished I
hadn't. There, lying curled around the centre pin of the record turntable
was a huge and perfectly formed turd! Oh no! I had 'given birth to an
otter' on top of six hundred quid's worth of Japanese technology. A dim
memory of getting up for a crap in the night came back to me. I decided
to lie. I denied everything and blamed it on one of the guests. Amazingly,
she believed me. But Justine, if you should ever read this, I am very, very
sorry, but it was me who shat on your stereo ...

NIGHTMARE ON 16TH GREEN
Winning golfer humiliated

Needing a crap on the way home from a day-time drinking session
with some college friends, I managed to persuade my boozing buddies
to take a short-cut across the golf course so I could have a dump on
their private, well-manicured lawns. However, much to the amusement
of my mates, I decided to squat over the hole on the 16th green and let
a perfect turd slip into the cup. We then retired to the safety of the trees
as a group of players appeared on the horizon. They played up to the
green, and met with our polite applause as they neared the hole and their
final putts. Finally, the star player, with much posturing, sank his putt,
and strutted over to the hole to smugly retrieve his winning ball. Then
everything seemed to go into slow motion as he knelt down, still
grinning at the crowd, lowered his hand into the hole and slowly
withdrew his ball. As he looked down, his face became confused, then
contorted, as he realized that his hand, and his ball, were speckled with
smudges of shit. He didn't even have the decency to yell 'Fore!' as he
threw caution to the wind and launched the brown-stained projectile
at the cackling drunks who were by now legging it through the rough.

PISS-UP GOES AWRY
Uncle's toilet trauma

My father used to meet up with his two brothers every year for the
Rugby League Challenge Cup final at Wembley. One year, after watching
the match, they went to a pub for a few bevvies. During the course of the
evening, my uncle came back from the toilets in a panic. He told my dad
and other uncle they had to drink up and leave at once. They did this,
and while looking for another pub, my dad demanded an explanation. My
uncle talked of that moment when your eyes get accustomed to the dark
and things become clearer. Well, he'd just been to the toilet and it was
dark there, so he pissed against the wall, knowing the urinals had to be
there somewhere. As his eyes became accustomed to the dark, however,
he noticed a TV in the corner of the room, then a dressing table
appeared, then a bed, then, finally, the stark realization that he was
pissing against the wall of the landlord's bedroom.

GOLDEN SHOWERS
Mates get unwelcome drenching

One hot day last year I went to an all-day music festival with a bunch of mates. Because of the enormous crowd it took ages to fight our way to the front for the best view. Unfortunately, because we had spent the entire morning drinking, by the time we were in pole position we were all desperate for a pee. Unwilling to lose our hard-won vantage point we were resigned to spending the next few hours in agony, until one bright spark realized that we could piss into our now empty plastic beer glasses and then drop them over the other side of the crowd barrier. Bladders now emptied, we relaxed to enjoy the bands. Unluckily for us, as the sun grew hotter the security guards began to work their way along the barrier, throwing pints of water onto the parched crowd. Far too late for us to escape we realized that this water was also in plastic pint glasses, placed strategically behind the crowd barrier. We stood helpless and unable to move as the bouncers got to where we were and threw seven pints of warm, fresh piss all over us.

NIGHT BUS INCIDENT
Sneaky drunk caught out

A few months ago, having been out for a few drinks with some friends, I decided to catch the bus home. As I strolled to the bus stop I saw the bus coming – there's only one an hour at that time of night – and dashed to catch it. Luckily the driver waited for me and I boarded the bus. I sat down in a seat next to a group of fairly drunk girls, and before long I was desperate for a pee. There was no way I was getting off and waiting another hour for a bus, so I tried to think of other things. The girls got talking to me and I found myself in the odd position of having to control my bladder while I was being chatted up. Every bump, corner and sudden stop was a nightmare as I strained to control my bladder. Finally, I had a bright idea. I pulled out my fags and made my way to the top deck. Luck! Nobody was up there, so had a long, joyous pee, taking care to put my jacket over the driver's spy-mirror. I zipped up and went downstairs, only to be sworn at, pushed and hit by the previously friendly girls. What I didn't know was that there were drains on the top deck, and my pee had gone down one and back in the sliding window – all over the girls.

SHOWER REFUGE
Lovers come out fighting

While out on a session, a mate and I pulled two nice looking ladies, and went back to their house for what promised to be a great night. I ended up in the kitchen getting the best blow job of my life, when there was a knock at the door. My girl looked up at me in complete horror – it was her boyfriend, so my mate and I were dispatched to the bathroom to wait for him to leave. We stood there for half-an-hour – me holding a bottle of shampoo as a defensive weapon, and my pal clutching a soap-on-a-rope – until we heard grunting from downstairs. We crept down to be greeted by the sight of a man-mountain giving my bird the best shag of her life. The guy could clearly hurt us, so we scuttled back to the bathroom. Ten minutes passed, and we heard footsteps on the stairs. The door burst open, and in walked the man, naked. Failing to notice us, he started having a piss. Knowing that as soon as he finished he would turn and see us, we looked at each other, nodded, and charged him. I twatted him around the head with the shampoo and my mate slapped him around the arse with the soap. We charged down the stairs and out the door, pausing only to look back at a redbottomed man, staring at us in utter disbelief.

FROTHY PINT
Poodle flavours ale

While in Gibraltar with the navy, some friends and I decided to go out on a sightseeing trip. We were joined by an old steward – all tattoos and no teeth – who had invited himself along. While we were having a few beers in a café, our sweaty guest suddenly nipped off to the bar and returned with some cheese and onion crisps. He didn't eat them however, and it was only when one of the lads went for a pee that their purpose became apparent. Having opened the pack, he beckoned over the owner's poodle. Then, while the dog happily munched away, the dirty sod reached down and started to toss it off. With a little whimper the dog finally shot his puppy paste, which the steward promptly scooped into our man's pint. Having been ordered not to say a word, we could only stare in disbelief when our pal returned and downed his poodle-top beer in one. To this day I finish my pint before going to the toilet.

WATER-GUN PRANKS
Party-goer ingests urine

On Christmas Day in 1995, I was lucky enough to find myself on the other side of the world, in Sydney, Australia. Twenty-five or so close friends and I were enjoying a marvellous barbecue in the sweltering weather, complete with cold beers and plenty of party games. One girl, Liz, who had drunk enough Castlemaine XXXX to stun the Wallabies, amused herself for several hours by running around with a high-powered water rifle, and took great delight in shooting powerful jets of water at unsuspecting friends. This was quite funny for an hour or two, but pretty soon people began to get a bit tired of having their beer and backs watered down every five minutes. Eventually I snatched the watergun off her, leaving her to find some other form of amusement. I then took the rifle into the khazi and filled it with piss. Back at the barbie, I set about finding the original shooter, who, when I tracked her down, proved to be a good sport. Instead of running away she simply lay down on the grass, laughing. She urged me to 'fill her up' and opened her mouth. Needless to say, I complied, and directed a hot, high-powered jet of pee straight into her wide open mouth. Revenge has perhaps never been sweeter, although Liz left the following day for Tasmania.

TOE TROUBLE
Camper's 'bath'

Back in the mid-Nineties I was asked to go camping by mates, sharing a tent with my girlfriend. We happy campers had a great first night, drinking copiously around the fire in a field in the middle of nowhere. Once we'd retired to my tent, my girlfriend got the horn, and after drunkenly undressing we were soon at it like rabbits, before dropping off into a booze-fuelled sleep. Naturally, I awoke a few hours later dying for a piss, so wandered out into the darkness to take a leak. On my return I found my girl awake and ready to go again – and as that ginger sponger Fergie was all over the papers at the time, she treated me to five minutes of toe-sucking. Next morning we awoke to a dreadful smell, prompting my girlfriend to quit the tent in search of breakfast. I then peeled back the sleeping bag to find both my feet encrusted in dried cow-shit from my small-hours ramble. Except, of course, the one big toe my missus had lovingly caressed the night before.

PUB LUNACY
Regular desperate for pint

About ten years ago I worked as a barman in one of Bolton's roughest pubs. There was nothing the regulars wouldn't do for a drink, and during my time there I saw men drink their own piss and scoff horse shit. The worst moment came when one of the locals bet another that he wouldn't eat a handful of maggots for a pint. The chap agreed, and after a quick trip round to the fishing tackle shop, an ashtray of maggots was produced. The cheers went up, the maggots went down, and the pint was won. But it didn't end there. The next day the maggot eater came bursting out of the toilet and demanded we went and had a look. Amazingly, some of the little buggers had made it right through his system alive, and were wriggling round in the water. 'I bet you wouldn't eat them now,' one of the lads jokingly said to the man. He did.

ROMEO'S URINATION BLUNDER
Chaos in dark lavatory

In my first month at college I started going out with a girl and, after a while, the time came to meet Mum and Dad. A few pints were needed to help me pluck up the courage just to knock on the front door. A while later, brimming with beer and tea, I went to the bathroom, but could find neither a switch nor a cord to turn on the light. In the dark, I found the sink, into which I relieved myself, rather than wasting any more trouser-threatening seconds, then briefly ran the tap and merrily skipped downstairs. I soon noticed a distinct cooling of relations between me and this family. Glances were exchanged. No-one talked. My girlfriend, no longer holding my hand, sat at the far end of the settee. Having eventually said my goodbyes, I was hurried to the front door by my girlfriend, who said, 'Did you piss in the sink?' Then I realised – the plug! It must have still been in the plughole! That was the end of our relationship.

LUCRATIVE SICKIE
Skiver hits paydirt

A couple of years ago me and my flatmate worked for a large company organizing staff incentives, to which we invariably managed to invite ourselves. One such freebie involved taking 30 wage-slaves to a restaurant in London's Chinatown one Friday night. Due to the amount of alcohol I'd previously consumed I couldn't face any Chinese food, but nevertheless carried on drinking until I could hardly walk. The rest of the weekend consisted of hair of the dog, while my mate put his sickness and diarrhoea down to too much wine – but come Monday he was still doubled up in pain. I phoned work on his behalf, when my boss told me that 24 of the people who'd been out that evening had also called in with food poisoning, so naturally I jumped on the bandwagon and, hungover, claimed a couple of sick days myself. I left the company a year later, but three months ago I received a letter from my old employers stating that the Chinese restaurant had admitted responsibility for the food poisoning, and due to the distress were enclosing a cheque for £1,027.50. Now, every time I look at my new dining table and chairs, I happily recall the most profitable hangover I've ever had.

DRUNKEN HORROR
Zombie misses his stop

Several years ago, I was flicking through a listings magazine when I saw an advert for a club in Soho which was having a party to celebrate the release of the film *Return Of The Living Dead*, telling people to come dressed as zombies with the best zombie outfits getting in for free. Well, getting in the mood with a bottle of whisky and a bottle of port, a mate and I, with the help of my girlfriend, made ourselves up. For some reason I decided I would wear a skirt and blouse, and after covering ourselves in mud and flour and suitably ripping up our clothes, we staggered out into the night. Sadly, on arrival at the club, we found the party had been cancelled. Undeterred, we decided to get a few more bottles and do a tour of Soho. This went well, save for occasional bemused looks from passers-by. Later, at some hazy point, my mate chucked me onto a night bus. I fell asleep in the luggage compartment and woke up at half past eight the next morning in a shop doorway, with Saturday morning shoppers looking on in horror at the white-faced transvestite zombie with port-coloured puke all over 'herself'. I have to say I walked home in shame, some brave soul having robbed my pockets of my cab fare. Isn't it amazing how many of your neighbours clean their cars on a Saturday morning?

HOOKER CHUNDERS
Player struck by own mess

Several years ago my rugby team went on its annual coach tour of France. Our hooker at the time was notorious for his excessive booze intake, and by the time we reached Dover, he was ready to burst – which he promptly did, puking up his ring into an empty burger bag. Drunk and weak, he then shoved it up into the skylight and went to sleep. Mercifully, we travelled 120 km across France without further incident. When the coach arrived at our town, a small Renault cut us up at the lights, causing the bus driver to slam on the brakes. At that moment our hooker was walking back up the bus and was suddenly catapulted headlong down the aisle. The putrid, freezing carton of sick shot out of its resting place and twatted him straight in the face, exploding on impact. To cap things off, the stench caused another nine hardened players to puke into their laps.

WORK SKIVER
Man makes front page

Bunking off work one fine summer's day several years ago, I put my free time to good use by going on the piss with a couple of friends. We went into town nice and early, and got stuck into some serious drinking. As we staggered from pub to pub we got caught up with another gang of merry-makers, and they joined us in our drinking session. During the course of the afternoon I vaguely remember marching down the high street with a big gang of lads, laughing and shouting and generally having fun. I finally got home some time in the small hours, horribly drunk, but happy. At work the next day I used my hangover as cover, saying I'd had a 24-hour bug which left me bed-ridden. The smiles which greeted me left me suspicious, but it was only when I saw the front page of the local newspaper that I clicked that my drinking bender had been rumbled. There I was on the front page, a huge smile across my face, with a can of beer in one hand, arms slung around another couple of fellows, underneath the headline 'Gay rights march takes over city centre'.

EXIT ERROR
Vocal drinker silences bar

The Saturday before Wales played England in the first Six Nations Rugby championships, my wife and I decided to go on a bender in our local pub. After a heavy afternoon's drinking we had decided to head home, when it came to my attention that the England International, Garath Archer, had been leaning against my wife, inebriated. Being a passionate Welshman, and fired up by the forthcoming match, I spun around as we reached the exit, raised a triumphant arm and hollered 'Wales!' at the top of my voice.

Mortified by the sudden silence that ensued, my wife bundled me through the door, and it was then that we realized the extent of our mistake. Instead of the car park, we were, rather worryingly, standing in the gents toilets. When we emerged they were all waiting for us, and what felt like a hundred silent smirking faces watched our departure as we sheepishly shuffled through the crowd to the exit. Incidentally, England stuffed us a week later.

LIGHT BULB CRAZE
Experiment proves contagious

A few weeks ago, after a mind-melting Saturday night on the town, my mates and I headed home for a few vodka nightcaps. After sinking the best part of a bottle, one of the chaps suddenly informed us that if you force a light bulb into your mouth, its particular size and shape apparently forces your jaw to lock. Obviously one of us had to put this theory to the test, and sure enough, within 20 minutes, the four of us were in a taxi on our way to hospital to have a light bulb removed from a locked jaw. After queuing for several hours, we were finally seen by a sympathetic doctor who unscrewed the metal part of the bulb, inserted a small cloth and carefully smashed the glass. Fortunately, other than a sore mouth, my mate wasn't injured, so we headed for home. Just as we were leaving however, a sheepish-looking man walked in with a light bulb wedged in his mouth. It was none other than the same taxi driver who had driven us to the hospital four hours earlier.

SPEWING MISHAP
Rugby players sprayed

The bastard bolted out of nowhere and hammered into my jaw with the top of his skull, smashing it up and sending me straight to hospital. But there is a fine tradition in our rugby club. Even when sent to hospital, you're still expected to attend the post-match drinkfest – body-cast, crutches and all, if need be. My jaw was wired shut. It didn't hurt so much; my doctor knows some wonderful drugs. Despite the tangle of teflon wires, I could still part my lips enough to stick a straw into my mouth. I could drink! Four or five pints later, my mates had left me leaning against a wall, facing the dancefloor, when a strangely familiar taste began to creep into my mouth. Mere seconds passed before my stomach went into overdrive. I retched. Hard. But my clenched jaws refused to open. So, instead of blowing big chunks harmlessly to the floor, the pressure of the retching caused me to spray a fine mist of puke through my teeth, and giving it quite a distance. The hapless dancers in front of me soon realized what was happening and fled in all directions. It was like watching the victims of Pompeii in a vain attempt to escape the vile drizzle. When, at last, it seemed as if the rain of digestive juices and warm beer had ceased, the chunks that had lodged against the back of my teeth began to slither down my throat, causing me to barf anew. Any stragglers that had stayed behind were spewed again with fresh vomit. There was no more dancing after that.

FIRE FIGHTER
Have-a-go hero gets it wrong

In the summer of 1993, my friend – whom I'll refer to only as Corky – was considering applying to join the fire service. I was in the pub one night with Corky when a girl ran in shouting that there was a burning car outside. Corky, by now in a drunken stupor, seized his chance of gaining firefighting credentials and ran out to assess the situation. Through the plumes of smoke, Corky could just make out a figure slumped against the steering wheel. Ignoring the advice of boozed-up onlookers, he ran to the blazing car, opened the door and attempted to extract the driver. Suddenly, a fire engine arrived: two real firemen jumped out and struggled to remove my choking friend from the wreck. Corky was treated for smoke inhalation and second-degree burns, and was whisked off, unconscious, to the local hospital. Two hours later, he came round, expecting a hero's reception – only to discover that the 'body' was the driver's seat slumped forward, with a furry seat cover hanging from the 'head'.

ACADEMY REGURGITATION
Trainee copper leaves trail

A few years back, I decided to attend a police training course for my local constabulary. About 50 of us hopefuls were sent to a country retreat for a week; after tests during the day, we all went out and partied in the evening. One night, just before the course finished, I returned to my room, incredibly pissed, and crashed out on the floor. Next morning, rather worse for wear, the contractions started in my stomach and I knew I was about to honk, but as I didn't have time to make it to the toilet and I didn't want to mess up the room, I chucked up out of my fifth-floor window, then went to breakfast. As I entered the canteen, I spotted the chief instructor and ten recruits peering out of the window of the quadrangle at a commotion that was going on outside. Shitting myself, I looked out over the shoulders of the huddle, where I saw a swarm of flapping seagulls fighting over the choice cuts from my spew. Not only that, but there was a trail of sick over the outside ledge of the window to my room. Strangely, I never made it as a copper.

ROLLERCOASTER HURLING WORRY
G-force breakfast bother

It was my birthday and I had a stinking hangover from a heavy night's drinking, so I tried the traditional cure – a full English breakfast, washed down with a ceremonious pint of lager. Later, some friends were treating me to a free day at the infamous Liverpool show in Wavertree. We headed straight for the beer tent, sunk three pints and moved on to the rides. 'The Enterprise' was the first, a rollercoaster featuring a daring swoop from 30 ft, with a finale of death rolls. I was loving it, until the death rolls, when my breakfast and beer decided to part company with my stomach. It was like a scene from *Hellraiser II* or *The Exorcist*, I was a 360° human vomit spraying machine. I got off the ride slightly dazed, and staggered to the toilet to splash my face, where I saw a distinctly beefy man swearing and cursing by the wash basin. He shouted, 'Some bastard threw up over my new jacket.' He then noticed that I had vomit all over me, and his eyes narrowed in anger. Somehow able to think straight, I quickly said, 'Oh yeah? Me too!'

DRINKER UNLOADS
Driver fails to contain himself

Many years ago I attended a friend's stag party in London. All the usual shenanigans took place, but although there was many a tale of woe to be told the next morning, I somehow managed to avoid embarrassing myself. Rather pleased, I headed home, but trying to steer down the motorway made me realize that I was in no fit state to be in charge of a car, and by the time I reached Brighton I desperately needed to vomit. Pulling over on a quiet street, I hurriedly wound down the window and leaned out. Sadly, a pair of nice old pensioners, out enjoying a morning stroll, decided that I must be stopping to ask for directions, and approached the car with big smiles. They came right up, and in a frail, quivering voice, one asked 'Yes, dear?' And then, with a mighty roar, I disposed of a gutload of beer and carrots straight onto their feet. Desperate to get away from the hapless duo, I looked straight ahead, wound the window up, and drove off, pausing only to look in the rear-view mirror, where a pair of vomit-soaked old biddies stood side by side, waving angry fists.

FOOTBALL ERROR
Fans invade public house

I was watching the recent England vs Tunisia game with the lads in the pub, but after a couple of drinks we decided to switch venues, as the boozer we were in was getting more and more crowded. We left at half-time with England winning one-nil. After several failed attempts at finding a gaff with a bit of space and a TV, we finally stumbled upon a pub with the game on and a group of five or six people quietly drinking in the corner. Result! We went in, ordered our drinks and began watching. After ten minutes or so, full of beer and national pride, we started to get annoyed with the other group – they didn't seem bothered about our lads, even when we went two-nil up. We began shouting at them, including a relentless chant of 'Traitors! Traitors!' They simply ignored us, fuelling more and more vitriolic abuse. Finally, the barman came over and barred us! It seems we had somewhat upset a family mourning the death of a grandparent.

TRAINEE DRINKER'S ERROR
Two men in a bed

A few years ago, my main goal in life was to improve my drinking capacity. One evening, I had perhaps taken a little too much alcohol on board, and I was frankly paralytic. Bedtime that night at my girlfriend's place was a frosty affair. During the night nature called and I went to the bathroom, an achievement in itself. I kept the light off in the bedroom and carefully felt the bed to avoid crushing my girlfriend as I got back in. Barely had I made myself comfortable than the bedroom door opened and a shaft of light fell across the bed from the hallway. I looked up to see my girlfriend standing in the doorway with a look of total horror on her face. Not half as horrified as her 16-year-old brother did, though, crushed up against the wall after I had inadvertently staggered into the wrong bedroom and climbed into his bed! Needless to say, the relationship did not last long after that little gem.

BALLS-UP IN BOOZER
Dog shit causes punch-up

A few months ago, several friends and I were on a pub crawl. On entering one pub, we noticed a huge dog turd on the doormat and all walked over it – apart from my mate, Gumbo, who stepped into the stool and trod it into the pub carpet. About 15 minutes later four huge skinheads came into the boozer, and the largest of them seemed to be trying to wipe shit from his boots, much to the amusement of his three mates. Without thinking, Gumbo suddenly got off his stool and walked over to the gang of thugs. 'Oi, mate,' he said to the lead skinhead, 'I've just done that!' And he pointed at the shit on the skinhead's boot. The skinhead, obviously thinking Gumbo had shat on the pub doorstep, proceeded to twat him, breaking his nose.

MOTHER HEARS TOO MUCH
Lover presses wrong button

During a particularly heavy drinking session, I managed to pull an equally smashed young lady, through the simple technique of rubbing my crotch against her bottom. When the pub shut I walked her to the taxi rank, and while we had a little kiss, my mate punched her number into his phone. Then she jumped in a cab, and we walked home. On the way, we went into great detail as to what I would do to her the next time we met, and as my mate already knew her, he filled me in on what I could expect. A few days later I nervously called her, and found that things hadn't exactly gone to plan. After punching the number in, my mate had then accidentally pressed the dial button. Her mother was woken by a ringing phone, and answered to a couple of drunken louts describing the hard shagging her daughter was soon to receive, including various props, and perhaps the aid of unspecified fruit. Worse still, the daughter got home before us, and they put us on the speaker phone. Amazingly however, she was still very keen to meet up for another drink.

UNDERGROUND FIASCO
Pals' porno disaster

A few months ago I was in Soho on a Saturday-night bar crawl with my best mate. Passing a 'specialist literature' shop, my friend persuaded me to buy a publication that catered to both our sordid tastes. We then returned to the night's mission: drinking. After chucking-out time, we found ourselves in the Tube station racing each other down parallel escalators. Within seconds, we were travelling at 80 mph, taking 14 steps at a time and completely unable to stop. Reaching the bottom, my legs gave out and my mate also tripped – we both ended up in a heap on the ground. Everybody looked up. Meanwhile, a group of young girls seemed amused at finding that my jazz mag had flown out of my pocket during the tumble so that loads of naked women performing various lewd acts were splayed all over the platform. As the girls passed us, they smirked and started screaming, 'Happy wanking, boys!' as they headed up the escalator. Not a pulling stunt I'd particularly recommend ...

PHOTO BLUNDER
Drunk men exposed

Following a fairly heavy night on the booze, my friend Alex and I made our way to the station to catch our train home. Feeling pissed and merry, we decided to kill the 15 minutes' wait for our train by mucking about in the passport photo booth. We stuck our two quid in the machine, struck a variety of hilarious poses, then fell out and waited for the results of our work. Unfortunately, while we were waiting, my female boss came up and started a conversation. She was getting the same train as us, and stood chatting as the photo booth made ominous rumblings. Then our photos dropped out. She has never mentioned the episode at work, but I often wonder what she thought of the four pictures of me and Alex waving our todgers at the camera lens, and I still get the odd grin from other female members of staff.

FANCY-DRESS FIASCO
Guest feels a right tit

I had been trying to pull this bird for several weeks when I was invited to her fancy-dress party. Having long hair, I went for the easy option: grow a goatee, don a loin cloth and go as Jesus Christ. While breaking in my costume with a drink at the local, I was invited to a friend's house to 'assimilate' a 24-can pack of golden throat charmer. By now, I was convinced that I could walk on water and impress this girl with my divine powers. Clutching my cross (a nicked 'For Sale' sign), I rapped on the door and was greeted by the young lady. Shocked, she explained that her parents were ultra-devout Catholics, and the sight of me dressed as the Messiah could end the party. She advised me to play down the religious angle, but my mind was too bent by now to grasp this. So off I stumbled, into the throng. Later I approached a fellow prankster – some bloke in full drag with a massive pair of fake tits – and laid my hands on the knockers, commenting, 'Nice set, mate!' My joy turned to dismay: 'he' was a 'she', and my paws were squeezing a complete stranger's breasts. And no ordinary stranger. Suddenly her husband, the host, appeared. Sensing that my chances of a bunk-up with the now-enraged daughter were not too good, I said to the gentleman dressed as Yosemite Sam, 'Sorry, I thought she was a bloke.' Upon which the hostess became hysterical and I was asked, in no uncertain terms, to leave or pick a window.

STAG NIGHT CRUCIFIXION
Dead to the world

A few years ago I was best man at my mate's wedding. At the stag party, 20 or so close friends downed pints and chasers, then triple spirits with pint chasers. We were pretty far gone. After the pub closed, myself, the groom and two friends decided that a walk through the graveyard would be fun! Having been sick over one gravestone, the groom stumbled over to the door of the church and passed out. So we stripped him of all his clothes, lifted him up and tied him, stark naked, to a large stone cross. The next day, our antics gradually came back to me and I rushed to the church, where I found him still fast asleep, tied to the cross. I managed to untie him and get him dressed before he woke up. He thanked me for not embarrassing him the previous night – although he was puzzled as to why he woke up in a graveyard. The week after the wedding, an article appeared in the local paper about a young man having been seen naked in the graveyard that night. Word got round as to his identity – for which I received a black eye and a broken nose!

TELEPHONE ERROR
Student bores his girlfriend

Like many a feckless student, I recently spent most of my grant cheque in a single night's drinking at the Student Union. Not being a complete idiot I managed to stagger back to my room for some well-earned sleep in the early hours of the morning. I drank a pint of water and lay down on the bed. Naturally the whole room started swimming, so I stood up to try to work out how to kill some time to get rid of the dizziness. I decided to give my girlfriend a call. This was no simple matter as she was on her year out in India, I had no money, and my phone only took incoming calls. Remembering that my parents had said I could use their chargecard for emergency calls, I decided to put it to use. After several unsuccessful attempts I actually managed to get through and proceeded to have a drunken argument with my highly annoyed girlfriend, who quite rightly pointed out what a wanker and a bore I was. At this I terminated the call, staggered back to bed and crashed out. In the afternoon I woke up and saw the phone was off the hook. By sheer chance both my girlfriend and I had failed to hang up properly, resulting in a staggering 11-hour call between Newcastle and India. I haven't seen the bill yet.

TAKE-AWAY PRANK
Cruel scousers dupe pal

A couple of years ago, a group of us embarked on a stag night pub crawl in the Wavertree area of Liverpool. After getting the groom absolutely paralytic, we decided to go to an Indian restaurant to complete the night's events. But not long after the food arrived, Gordon, the groom, disappeared into the toilet – and failed to return. Eventually, my brother went in to see if he was alright; he returned with Gordon slung over his shoulder, so we put his curry in a doggie-bag and caught a taxi home. Ten minutes into the journey, Gordon announced that he was going to be sick, and – not wanting to face the wrath of an irate taxi driver – I decided it was best to sacrifice the dinner and gave him the bag, which he promptly filled. Our other friend, Robbie, had fallen asleep during the ride and missed the whole incident, so when we arrived at his front door and woke him up, I couldn't resist handing him the carrier bag, telling him that Gordon couldn't face it and that one of the containers had split, but that otherwise the food was okay. He took the bag and a few days later thanked me for the meal, proudly stating that he had polished the lot off and found it delicious, if a little mushy.

DISCO SHAME
Fighting on the dance floor

It started out as the usual Friday night: beers, chatting and eventually a club. The week in question me and a few mates went to a club which had just opened. We were fairly drunk but by no means bladdered, but we did decide to have a game of 'spoof' – a variation on the paper/rock/scissors game – with the loser having to do the forfeit of his mates' choice. After I lost a round I was instructed to go onto the half-filled dancefloor and dance like, for want of a better word, a spaz. I duly went down in front of the speakers and jerked around, dragging my leg behind me in terrible taste. After several minutes I felt a vicious punch to my cheek, and turned around to fight the bastard who'd hit me. We exchanged hard blows for a solid minute, then the bouncers came over and dragged me out. A minute or so later my friends came out to find me black and blue, sitting dejectedly on the kerb, our fun evening over. It was then that my mates pointed out the lad I'd fought sported an orthopaedic shoe.

TOILET TRAUMA
Graduate gets the wrong man

Following our graduation ceremony at Newcastle University, a group of friends and I went out to celebrate. Considerably the worse for wear, my friend Paresh and I zigzagged our way to the gents. Paresh, now out of his student gear and wearing some Cerruti slacks and Gucci cufflinks, went into the cubicle to avoid getting splashback on his expensive attire. What he didn't realize was that a huge Geordie bloke had followed us into the toilets and was standing next to me at the urinal. I finished my slash and went to wash my hands, while the Geordie, much to everyone's surprise, squeezed out a huge anal fanfare. 'You smelly fucker!' shouted Paresh from his cubicle, thinking I was the only one there. He then must have balanced himself on the rim of the bowl, because a jet of hot urine shot over the partition and all over our Geordie pal. I chose this moment to leave, just as the enraged bloke began to kick down the door of the cubicle. I returned to the toilets ten minutes later to find Paresh half-conscious in a pool of blood.

UNCOMFORTABLE PUDDING EVENT
Girlfriend caught with trifle

A few years ago, I was with my girlfriend at my best friend's sleep-over party. The vodka trifles I had made went down very well, and eventually everyone crashed out. I was woken by an excited friend dragging me towards the stairs telling me that there was a commotion going on outside. The house was on the side of a hill and the front door was upstairs. As I left the house I could see a circle of my friends peering through a window. As we got closer I could make out the master bedroom and a naked male arse atop a blonde girl. I was jeering and cheering along with the other voyeurs until I recognized the girl as being my girlfriend, the bloke as my best friend and my vodka trifle being licked off her bare breasts.

SOBER HUMILIATION

FLATULENCE FAUX-PAS
Love-object is scorned

When I was at college, I had it bad for a gorgeous Dutch girl. I spent
many lectures gazing longingly at the blonde, leggy Annika, but she never
even gave me a passing glance. I was living in halls at the time, in a small
box of a room. One night, as finals were approaching, I was holed up in
my bunker studying like crazy. With the door and window shut, I was
enjoying a good old farting session, ridding my body of the day's built-up
wind. Several violent emissions later, the room was shimmering in a haze
of noxious gas. Then suddenly there was a knock on the door and, before
I could leap up, the lovely Annika popped her head in and smiled
invitingly: 'Hi, are you busy?' I could do nothing but get her away as
quickly as possible. I shouted, 'Get out! How dare you barge in here
without knocking!' A look of horror struck her, and she turned and fled.
Needless to say, she went back to treating me with disdain.

THATCH SNIPPED
Man ruins meal with hidden horrors

About five years ago, I was sitting half naked in front of the TV, when
I discovered a large tangled knot in my pubes. I reached for some
scissors and snipped around the offending clump. Once done, I realized
I needed something to put the hairs into, so I grabbed a piece of paper,
and neatly folded the little bush away before putting it into my pocket
and staggering off to bed. A few days later I was in a restaurant having
lunch with three important clients. We discussed another client, and
I asked one of my contacts for his phone number, fumbling around for
a piece of paper to write it down on. Closely watched by my bemused

colleagues, I then meticulously unfolded my A4 sheet to reveal a neatly pressed pubic topiary display, which then blew straight into my colleague's chicken supreme.

SOUR GRAPES
Man fleeced for pricy plonk

Several years ago I found myself between flats, and a very close friend of the family agreed to put me up for a week or two while I sorted out a place to live. Everything went smoothly and I eventually found a new flat, and decided to buy a present for my kind host by way of a thank you. Knowing he was a bit of a wine buff I went down to the local off-licence to choose a decent bottle of wine. Too proud to ask advice from the man behind the counter, I eventually selected a bottle of red, thinking that the '£7.99' sticker on the shelf put it in the 'pretty good' range. I took the bottle up to the counter and the man seemed most impressed by my choice. He asked me if I had tasted it before, and I said yes. I lied that only a week before I had bought a bottle, and found it superb. He smiled and said that they didn't sell many because of the price, and I nodded knowingly, and said that it was worth every single penny. Then the man rang the till: '£47.99'. The '4' sticker had obviously fallen off the shelf. I was too embarrassed to backtrack though, so my friend ended up with the best leaving present ever.

BICYCLE BUNGLE
Cyclist gets a ticking off

I cycled into town for a 9 am appointment with fear – well, my dentist actually. When all the fillings were done, after about an hour, I rode to the shops, bought two cans of Whiskas for the cat and a bottle of Lucozade, and set off home to nurse my aching mouth. Two hundred yards from my door, I swerved to avoid a pothole and crashed into the kerb. I lay in the gutter, clothes torn, knees bleeding, with tins of Whiskas rolling down the street and a smashed bottle of Lucozade all over the pavement. I looked up to see an old woman peering over me. 'Are you okay, son?' she enquired. I nodded, staggered to my feet and opened my mouth to respond. All that came out was an incoherent 'zsa zsa zsa' as my mouth was still frozen from the dentist. Her concern evaporated into a cold look of disgust. 'It's a disgrace! Someone so drunk at 10 o'clock in the morning! You ought to be ashamed of yourself, young man. Serves you right!' I haven't been to see the dentist since.

'PHONE SEX' FAUX PAS
Caller compromises a friend

One night, having consumed too much alcohol and a greasy kebab, my mates and I retired to a friend's house to watch an 'adult' video. Struggling out of bed the next day, I decided to give one of the crew a ring. When he answered the phone, I began to repeat some of the dialogue from the film. 'Oooh, come on. Johnny, fuck me ... I want that big cock inside me ... that's it! Harder ... HARDER! You're so big!' The next thing I heard was the sound of a phone being slammed down; but, mysteriously, I could still hear my friend on the line, blathering away in a blind panic. His mother, a woman so strait-laced that she'd make Mother Teresa took like Tabatha Cash, had picked up the phone at the same time downstairs. So Mrs M, if you come across this piece, it was me who made the obscene phone call, and I'm sorry if you've spent years in torment about the sexual activities of your favourite son.

BOARDING SCHOOL BLUNDER
Secret drinker blows it

As a young man at a mixed boarding school, I, like many others, turned to drinking to cheer up the mind-numbing dullness of the routine. Naturally, storage of the illicit sauce was a problem, as privacy is not one of the benefits of a private education. Then one day I hit upon a novel hiding place: the inside of my stereo speaker-case. To combat the clinking of bottles, I packed out the spare space with empty plastic bags and toilet paper. I could even play music as the teachers searched for the booze. One day just such a hunt occurred, and I casually flicked through the tracks on my CD as the teacher looked through the dorm. He found nothing, and we both left, me to go to chapel for two hours and he to continue his search. Returning to my dorm after chapel, I could smell smoke as I walked upstairs. Looking across the room as I entered, I saw the gin-filled speaker explode like a Molotov cocktail. Then the curtains caught fire and the room filled up with thick smoke. It seems a short circuit had ignited my padding and sent the whole lot up. Needless to say, I was well and truly rumbled.

CELEBRITY TROUSER TORMENT
Large thighs dilemma

A few years ago I worked for a menswear shop which specialized in hiring out dress suits for weddings. The Solent athletic team all came in to get fitted one afternoon. While I started measuring one tall black guy, he mumbled something about having big thighs and said he would need extra size trousers. I ignored him, knowing most men don't know their true sizes. I gave him 32-inch trousers and he disappeared into the changing room. After a minute, he reappeared with his trousers at half mast, clearly unable to pull them up over the most muscular thighs I have ever seen. He ended up with 38-inch trousers, which had to be held up with braces, making him look like Coco the Clown. He was very annoyed by now, and when I took his name, I wrote it down as 'Kriss Akapussy'. 'No, Aka-BUSI,' he shouted. I could hear my colleague giggling behind me. Needless to say, I never did watch much athletics on TV.

CAR REPAIR BACKFIRES
Mechanic rues experiment

When I was 17, my dad bought me my first car: a Mini 1000. Already 15 years old, it looked knackered, but for £150 it was a great deal. As part of my present I had the car sprayed British Racing Green, which made it look better, but its rusty wheels and old fashioned hubcaps let it down. Unable to afford alloy sports wheels, I decided to spray the existing crappy wheels silver and get rid of the hubcaps. I dismantled the wheels and got to work with a can of silver spray, noticing in the process that each wheel-nut had a straight side and a rounded side. The rounded side, I thought, was far sportier, so I sprayed the wheels silver with the rounded sides on show. Later, after half an hour or so on the road, I heard a grinding noise that was getting louder with every corner. On inspection I decided it was just a teething problem from my new design, but while I was taking a right turn at speed the grinding noise came back, louder than ever, with sparks flying past the window. The car sank 12 inches with a great thud. I ground to a halt with a worried look on my face as the two front wheels made their own way home – unattached.

COOL DRIVING BLUNDER
Jilted man in getaway farce

My first serious girlfriend dumped me on Christmas Day. I'd driven to the house she shared with her mother to deliver her presents, and she broke the news in a typically blunt way. Distressed beyond words, I ran out to my car and decided I'd depart in a dramatic and memorable fashion. I jumped into my beaten-up Escort and attempted a fast-moving reverse flick out of her narrow driveway. Unfortunately, instead of flying backwards in a cloud of burning rubber, I deposited my car into her mother's prize flower bed. This was bad enough, but, in my frantic attempt to escape before anyone noticed, the spinning back wheels dug themselves deeper into the soil. My now ex-girlfriend's mother attempted to push the car out. She then remembered she was asthmatic and quietly collapsed on the driveway. To make matters worse, I had to borrow £75 from her to pay for a tow truck – I'd spent all my money on the Christmas presents. It transpired my 'ex' was meeting her new boyfriend that night, and was unable to get her car past the wreckage of mine, which was blocking the driveway.

HARD-TO-GET BLUNDER
Gay act is too convincing

When I was 20, I had no luck with women. Every time I spoke to a prospective girlfriend, I froze. I stuttered, spluttered, and generally made a complete fool of myself. Girls, using the uncanny sixth sense that only they have, sensed my hopelessness and gave me a wide berth. But all that changed when I met Julia. With gorgeous long red hair and snow white skin, she looked like she had just stepped out of a Pre-Raphaelite painting. I was determined not to mess this one up, so I came up with a cunning plan. Having read somewhere that girls liked a challenge and were attracted to the kind of blokes they couldn't have. Unfortunately, I got slightly carried away, and I thought I would be guaranteed success if I played even harder to get. So I told her I was a homosexual.

This didn't put her off. She invited me out the following night, saying she would 'arrange something very special' for me. I'd done it! I pictured the evening: Julia would introduce me to the love of a woman, I'd lie there, pretending to experience for the first time the unexpected pleasures of heterosexual love.

I turned up early, to find Julia already there. I was shaking in anticipation. She looked me in the eye, and said: 'Rick ... meet Gerald.' I froze, confused. Gerald stepped forward, looking like a refugee from the Village People. A leer broke out underneath the bushiest moustache I've ever seen. His shaved head glistened in the moonlight as he strode purposefully towards me, his black leather trousers squeaking. I turned and ran. Needless to say, I never saw Julia again.

TEA WITH MILK?
Student recycles waste

While in my first year at university, I suddenly found myself extremely hard up, and so were my student housemates. As anyone who has shared a house will know, a certain amount of 'borrowing' of one another's food goes on. Normally I took this stoically, but as I was trying to live on £1.38 per week, I found I could bear it no longer. I had put up with it for several weeks, but the final straw came when someone in my house all but finished my carton of milk. Returning home drunk and looking forward to my evening meal (and lunch and breakfast) of Frosties, I found the milk was almost all gone. I hit the roof. Determined to teach the culprit a lesson, I pissed in the carton and went to sleep, still seething. I was awoken at midday by one of my housemates saying my parents had just arrived to visit. 'I made them a cup of tea, I used your milk,' she said. I had trouble facing my parents after that, especially since my father crashed the car while being violently sick on the drive home.

DAIRY PRODUCE FIASCO
Innocent aunt humiliated
My aunt used to work part time as a typist for the Inland Revenue
in Manchester, where she took it in turns with the other girls in the
office to buy breakfast. One day she wandered into the butty shop,
ordered the usual buttered teacakes and put them into her bag – right
on top of a pair of underpants my uncle wanted returning to Marks
and Spencer because he didn't like the colour. My aunt then went into
M&S and took the pants to the till for exchange. 'Has he tried them
on?' the girl on the till asked. My aunt said absolutely not, then looked
on in horror as the assistant held the pants up to the light – and a bright
yellow streak was plain to see. The assistant refused to give my aunt a
refund, saying that it was quite clear the pants had been worn, as they
were 'soiled'. In a last, desperate attempt to preserve her dignity, my
aunt said in a very timid voice, 'It was only butter, you know ...'

NAMES ENTERED
Church remembers alive folk
On Remembrance Sunday last February, myself and a few friends
decided to attend a small memorial service at a nearby village church.
When we arrived, we filled in the visitors' book sitting in the foyer,
purely because judging by the neatly printed surnames, everyone else
in our small community had already entered their names. The service
went very well until the padre began to read out the village dead, and
we recognized the book he was reading from. Before he could get to
our neatly printed names however, my friend cracked, turned to me
and blurted out, 'We are going to hell for this, mark my words!' before
bolting for the door. I just followed, shrugging my shoulders and tutting
at the padre. We later found out that our names were indeed read out,
and not one person noticed.

SAUNA SAGA
Novice learns the hard way

About 12 years ago, when I was an innocent 26-year-old, my brother-in-law joined a posh local health club and took me along one evening as a special treat. After a work-out in the gym he suggested a sauna, so I stripped off and followed him in. The sauna was empty and I settled down on the top row, taking the small bowl of water that he handed to me. When I asked what it was for, he explained that the body needs to adjust to the sauna's high temperatures, and that your testicles are susceptible to heat damage. Now this seemed plausible, as I knew from biology 0-level that your balls were the coolest part of your body, so I positioned myself in such a way that I could sit with my nuts floating on the water. After a while, a couple of blokes strolled in, carrying the same bowls, and poured the contents over the hot coals. I was about to suggest that they save a little for their balls, when my brother-in-law suddenly cracked up and left, leaving two smirking men to explain correct sauna etiquette.

SELFISH GYM-GOER
Sauna causes sap to rise

Last April, after completing a strenuous work-out at my local gym,
I decided to spend a relaxing half-hour in the sauna. It had a lockable
door with a large tinted glass window, the other side of which was the
men's showers. Feeling selfish, I put the lock on and lay down to enjoy
a bit of solitary sweating. An old chubby man then wandered into the
showers and, after trying the sauna door, stood under a jet of water. I
left him to it and closed my eyes until it was time to leave. When I
opened my eyes however, I couldn't help but notice the old boy having
the best wank of his life. Worse, he was marvelling at his reflection in
the door window. Then he suddenly waddled straight over and, with only
a thin sheet of glass between my head and his angry Jap's eye, unleashed
a thick torrent of gentleman's gel all over the window. I waited a good
hour before I dared come out.

WEDDING FAUX PAS
Smoking bloke misses his cue

A couple of years ago, I was asked by my flatmate if I would help out at
her wedding. My job was simple: all I had to do was pick out a track on a
CD, press the button, and watch as the beautiful bride walked down the
aisle with her father to be given away. She was due at three o'clock, so at
2.45 I nipped outside for a quick cigarette with a couple of the ushers, all
the while keeping an eye on the path to the entrance so that I could rush
back in and put on the music when her car pulled up. After about 15 to
20 minutes, I started to get a bit concerned about her lateness, so
thought I'd better go inside and check what was going on. As I pushed
open what I was later told was the side entrance to the church, I was
greeted by the strange sight of my flatmate walking down the aisle with
a furious took on her face ... to the tune of *Mr Boombastic*. Nobody had
a clue what track to play, and when they couldn't find me, somebody had
just hit the play button. To cap it all, I accidentally caught the bouquet
later on in the day.

BLASPHEMOUS BROTHER
Unsuspecting caller insulted

Last year I visited my sister for the weekend. We were chatting on Sunday afternoon when she told me that the Jehovah's Witnesses had been coming round week after week, and just didn't seem to take no for an answer. As we drank our coffee there was a knock at the door, and I told my sister I would deal with it. Sure enough, there on the doorstep was a clean-cut young chap with an armful of books. Before he could begin to bore me with his chatter I told him, quite loudly, to fuck right off, and slammed the door in his face. Seconds later there was another knock at the door, and I went back to answer it. 'Look, mate,' I said, 'I've told you once. Now do yourself a favour and fuck off.' The young man remained very calm, although I noticed he turned rather red, and said: 'I'm the curate of St Cuthbert's Church, and am just checking to see that Vikki's (my niece) christening was satisfactory.'

HAIR MISHAP
Short shrift & shades

My hair was much too long for the hot weather so I heated myself up even more by going to one of those saloons staffed by Claudia Schiffer lookalikes. I was shown to a seat by a luscious blonde. I removed my sunglasses as she put a gown over my shoulders and I started cleaning them, beneath the gown. Before I could say 'short sharp crop' she screamed, 'You dirty bastard!' and yanked off the gown to reveal my now clean pair of sunglasses.

GRAFFITI VICTIM
Organist fails to check mirror

When I was a student at music college I took the job of organist at the local church in order to make a few quid at the weekends. The pay for Sunday services was abysmal, but it was easy to make up for this by doing the occasional wedding and funeral service. One Friday night I got completely out of it with my mates down the pub, which ended up in a session that lasted nearly all night. I eventually crashed out at around seven in the morning, with the promise from my mates that they would wake me up in time for a wedding service I had to perform the next day. Being the reliable bastards they are, they woke me up about 15 minutes before the ceremony. I chucked my clothes on and ran down to the church, where – luckily – the procession was only just making its way in. With a big smile I pushed my way through the crowd, saying 'Make way for the organist!' I sat down at my organ and, surprisingly, played the music without fault. Afterwards I went up to the vicar and apologized for being late, but he looked at me with an expression of total horror. 'You played well,' he said with a bright red face. 'It's just that you have the words "EVIL BASTARD" written on your forehead in lipstick.'

BLIND DATE DILEMMA
Don't fancy yours much

After splitting up with my girlfriend, I decided it would be a laugh to reply to some personal ads. One was from a 39-year-old woman after a young man for a fling. After we exchanged several explicit letters and steamy phone calls, she said we should meet. When we finally did I realized I made a big mistake. She'd described herself as slim and attractive, but was short, plump and had more arse than a donkey. After we'd spent about half an hour in a pub, I realized that I must escape. I went into the Gents but all the windows had bars on them. I waited until she went to the toilet, leaving me to took after her expensive coat and designer umbrella. After about a minute, I calmly walked out of the pub, then ran like an Olympic sprinter. Losing my way I asked directions to the nearest tube and felt a huge wave of relief as I saw an Underground sign in the distance. Then horror struck. Across the road was the pub I'd just escaped from. What followed was a scene of complete chaos as I ran through the crowds shouting, 'Get out of the way!' Thankfully, I never saw her again.

WATER FEAR
Natural obstacle spooks caver
The last caving expedition that I went on involved an unexpected 'sump' – a point where rock meets water. This particular obstacle was four foot long, and the only way past was to dive into the icy water and pull myself along a permanently fixed length of submerged rope. Easy enough, perhaps – except that I can't swim. Amazingly, however, I managed it, and enjoyed a full day's caving without incident. On the return leg, I again arrived at the ominous sump, and three of my mates dived under before tugging on the rope – the signal for me to go. I held my breath, screwed up my eyes and ducked underwater, frantically pulling my way to safety. As soon as I thought I was clear I raised my head, only to hit rock. I pulled myself further forward and tried again. More rock. Starting to panic, I made one last, desperate effort to save myself from drowning. To my amazement, I burst out of the water – only to be surprised to find that I was 20 ft from the sump and completely alone. My mates later told me that when I appeared from under the rock, they had stood either side of me and held a large boulder over my head, keeping pace with me as I dragged myself along the rope – before eventually adopting the 'scatter and divide' method to avoid a serious beating from a very scared caver.

ACCIDENTAL INSULT
Dropped book ends friendship
Recently I moved into a lovely new flat in a really great part of London, and had to find new flatmates. Luckily I found three super people, one of whom was a gentle German giant named Otto. After a few weeks in our new home I got round to putting up some bookshelves, and began the task of carrying all my books down to put them on the nice new shelves. I loaded up my arms and made my way down to the living room, where Otto was enjoying a cup of tea. Unfortunately, I tripped and dropped a couple of volumes at Otto's feet. I couldn't work out why the chap looked so horrified until I looked down at the heavy historic tome nestling against Otto's slipper: a copy of *Hitler's Willing Executioners*, an academic study about the collective guilt of the German people. Otto moved his stuff out three days later.

HOLE UNDAMMED
Elderly chubster enjoys motion

During the early Seventies I found myself in hospital with two broken legs. In the bed next to me lay a fat old man, who was in for chronic constipation. Every day after dinner, some poor nurse would have to stick a hose up his arse so that he could pass solids. Obviously this made him very irritable, so I used to rub salt in the wound with a cheerful announcement of, 'That was a great crap!' whenever I used the bedpan. The time came when I was finally allowed to leave, and I told the old boy that I would miss watching his daily hour of discomfort. He grumpily informed me that he needed a shit, but before I could summon a nurse, someone had a heart attack in the corner, and everyone scooted away to help. All alone, he pushed his generous arse out off the bed, until I was within kissing distance of it, and proceeded to empty his bowels onto the floor in front of me. A humungous pile of brown, black and red shit rose up off the tiles, and when he had finished he pulled his arse back in, turned to me with watering eyes and said, 'What a great crap that was!'

LIBRARY LAUGHS
Red face after security alert

Last year at university I competed in a practical joke tit-for-tat campaign with my friends. One day, while in the library with my mates Steve, Wayne and his girlfriend Lisa, Steve and I thought it would be amusing to remove a magnetic security strip from a book and plant it on Wayne. This we duly did, slipping it in his jacket pocket, knowing the security alarm and Secret Police-inspired librarians would provide adequate amounts of embarrassment. When the alarm went off and Wayne was asked to empty his bag for inspection, he became agitated and refused. Following a lengthy argument while Wayne proclaimed his innocence, he was finally persuaded to let the librarian look in his bag. She pulled out a magazine, believing it to be a stolen periodical – but the naked girl on the cover confirmed it was *Razzle* rather than *Business Week*. Wayne duly turned red and his girlfriend stormed off. They split up later that day and Wayne still hasn't forgiven us.

KITCHEN HORROR
Secret ingredient destroys love supper

Last year I was lucky enough to meet a beautiful girl at a party. I was even luckier when the girl – a model I had thought to be well out of my league – actually seemed to enjoy my company. Fully seizing the one and only opportunity in my life to make it with a stunner, I spent every second of the evening with her, and was shocked when my invitation to come to supper the following week was accepted. She told me she was a vegetarian and I spent the week devising the perfect meal. But while I was cooking my winter vegetable casserole I realized I didn't have any vegetable stock, so I bunged in a chicken stock cube, seasoned the whole thing heavily and prayed she wouldn't notice my deception. All went well. She ate a huge portion and complimented me on my cooking. When I asked her how long she had been a vegetarian, she told me it had only been for a year and that she actually loved meat but had developed a severe allergy to animal fat, breaking out in hives every time she ate it. Sure enough, as the evening passed her face broke out in blotches and she began to get feverish. In the end I had to confess. Due to her state she missed a modelling assignment the next day, and has never spoken to me since.

MORONIC MOTORIST
Man has car cock-up

Last July I was staying with my girlfriend for the weekend when I had a slight problem with my car. This would not have been so much of a drama, except that I only noticed the problem on Sunday afternoon, and I had to be at work, 150 miles away, early on Monday morning. I went into a blind panic when I noticed that fluid had leaked out all over the back wheels, and, taking the car for a careful test I felt that the brakes weren't responding as well as they should. I telephoned my boss, telling him the problem, and he was not at all impressed. On Monday morning I drove the car at a steady 15 mph to the nearest garage, and asked them to check the brakes for me. After a couple of hours I noticed the mechanics were laughing at me, then the manager called me over and told me my car was fine. After I'd returned home I received a letter from the garage which did nothing to placate my boss. It read: 'After a lengthy investigation of stripping and checking the front and rear brakes, it was determined that the fault was dog urine on the wheels'.

LAUNDRY SLIP-UP
Doting mother takes affront

Until recently, I had managed to enjoy a rather appealing washing arrangement, whereby I would take my work clothes around to my mother to be cleaned while my girlfriend would take care of my everyday stuff. A few weeks ago, however, mum started to visit my flat on an almost daily basis, and began taking all my washing – including my girlfriend's 'share' – when she left. Feeling unneeded, my girlfriend decided to lay down a few ground rules: namely that I should refer to her as 'Mammy' and let her do her fair share of the laundry. Over the next few weeks, she would bring round my clean clothes and say, 'Your Mammy is looking after you, isn't she, love?' 'Yes, Mammy, you are,' I would reply. One morning, after a particularly sordid sex session, I slipped out of bed and went to work without disturbing her. Later that day – at work – the phone rang, and a woman's voice said, 'It's your Mammy.' Smiling, I thanked the caller for the night before and asked her if there was any soreness in her nether regions. There then followed a steady silence, before the caller informed me that she'd decided to have a break from my father, that she was going to stay with my sister and that she wouldn't be able to do my washing for a while.

STORE DRAMA
Biker bothers shopper

When I was younger I was into motorbikes in a big way, and after yet another strip-down of my 50cc, I headed down to my local dealer to order some parts. While I was standing in the queue, dreamily watching the young girl working behind the counter, one of the shop dummies, complete with helmet, boots, jacket and gloves, fell over. The young shop assistant quickly came over and picked it up, and we had a laugh about it while I ordered my parts. Returning the next day to collect them I took my place behind a mean-looking man, who was dressed as if he had just stepped off the set of *Mad Max*. Again I soon found myself staring at the shop assistant, completely lost in thought, when suddenly the biker in front of me moved. Unfortunately, I had a sudden flashback to the previous day – and before I knew what I was doing I reached forward and grabbed him tight round the stomach. We wrestled for quite a long time before I came to my senses; all I could muster as I looked into his furious eyes was: 'Sorry, I thought you were a dummy.' Not surprisingly, I've never been back.

TATTOO SCREW-UP
Man scarred forever

For several years I had wanted a tattoo, but never liked a design enough to make the commitment. Then, last year, a Japanese student attended the college I go to, and we became friends. I introduced him to the lads, and we all had a great year. When he had to leave, he gave each of us a beautifully designed card with the Japanese characters of our names printed on them. My name looked really cool in Japanese script, so I decided to tattoo it on my shoulder. Everyone said how great it looked, and I was really pleased ... until I went to Sicily this April, when I took the opportunity to show off my tat on the beach. We were challenged to a game of volleyball by some Japanese girls who kept screaming 'Sidney!' at me – which was odd, as it's my best friend's name. Yep, the cards had been switched, and I now have my mate's stupid name scrawled across my shoulder.

BED DEPARTMENT VIOLENCE
Sleeping mammal awakens

I was recently shopping at a large local furniture store with two friends of mine, Jimmy and Dave. We'd previously spent a few hours in the pub and were in a pretty mischievous mood as we made our way around the beds, wardrobes and tables. It was in the bedding department that the mishap occurred. One brand of bed had been running TV ads featuring a hippo lying on a bed next to a tiny chick – the idea was that the bed wouldn't cause two people to 'roll together'. The shop had the bed on display, with a tiny stuffed chick and a giant hippo lying next to each other.

Jimmy ran over and booted the chick across the floor, then landed a roundhouse on the side of the hippo's head. Startlingly, the hippo rolled off the bed and cried: 'What the fuck did you do that for?' Jimmy had smacked a man whose job it was to dress up as a semi-aquatic mammal. Luckily, the sight of a blue hippo squaring up to Jimmy was so funny that we all ended up rolling around in laughter.

FILTHY KIWI
Bloke leaves his mark on bed

After leaving university I moved into a flat with a group of friends – one of whom I was pretty keen on. We had been in the flat a couple of weeks and I felt I was making good headway. One night a few of us, including the girl I fancied, were sitting around in my room chatting and having a few drinks. Trying to be laid-back and cool I was wearing an ilavalava – a Samoan version of the kilt, worn by both men and women. After a while we ran out of drinks and I volunteered to go to the local boozer to get more. I figured nobody wanted a shot of my balls as I stood up, so I slid delicately across the bed. On coming back with the beers I saw that the two blokes in the room had tears of mirth running down their faces, while the two girls were ashen-faced. I also noticed a book sitting in the middle of the bed. I picked it up and was shocked and embarrassed to find that, while sliding off the bed, rather than keeping my dignity I managed to lose it all by leaving a 4-inch shit stain on the duvet. I did, eventually, get it on with my flatmate, but it took four weeks of hard work to put the memory of the fudge strip firmly out of her mind.

SAMARITAN ATTACKS
Man breaks granny's face

During a recent lunchbreak, my mate and I nipped out to the local sandwich shop to grab a bite to eat. On the way back we noticed an old lady walking along the busy street with a bit of white paper stuck to her shoe. Ever the gentleman, my mate stepped forward and placed his foot firmly on the paper, the idea being that her next step would pull off the offending article. Unfortunately, it must have been literally nailed into place, because her foot suddenly stopped and she went face first into the pavement. Naturally we legged it, but there were obviously some outraged bystanders, as that weekend the local rag ran an amazing 'old lady attacked in broad daylight' story.

TOWERBLOCK SHOCKER
Man ignores noisy motorist

A few months ago I returned from a trip to Australia, and was totally jet-lagged by the time I arrived back at my flat in London. I'd crashed out for no longer than an hour before I was woken by a loud, repeated car horn. I live on the seventh floor of a tower block, so went onto the balcony to investigate. Down on the street below I could make out a Ford Mondeo and its occupant. The man was sitting in the driver's seat, hitting the horn and shouting 'Alfie! Alfie!' over and over again. I shouted down at him to shut up, but he just continued to blow the horn and yell out for his mate Alfie. I was tired and stressed out, so I ran into the kitchen and grabbed a carton of eggs from the fridge. I was so angry, I hurled the whole carton down at the car. The eggs splattered on the Mondeo's windshield, but the man kept up his stream of nonsense. Finally I snapped and chucked a milk bottle down, which smashed on his roof. At last, the noise stopped. I saw two men come and bundle the bloke out of his car: they had obviously been as pissed off as me. I went back to bed and slept for the next 16 hours. Only the next day did the full story emerge in the local press: the man in the car had suffered a heart attack, and was pressing his horn and shouting 'Help me! Help me!'

HOUSE ARREST
Ginger man stuns visitors

Back in 1993 I purchased my first house, a great open-plan affair with a gallery bedroom overlooking the living room. It had been one of the estate's showhouses, along with the adjoining house, which was still on display. During my first few months of residence I was subjected to countless numbers of people peering through my window, only to realize their mistake when they saw either myself or my girlfriend watching the

TV or having dinner. On the odd occasion when I was gardening, people would even walk up to the front door and peek in. Although it was amusing at first, it soon became a bit annoying – until the final straw, which followed a hard night shift. Having crawled into my bed at around 7 am, I was woken at 10.30 by my concerned girlfriend who was whispering insistently that someone was downstairs, walking around. Still half asleep, I mumbled something and dozed off, until she pushed me out of the bed, telling me that someone was now coming up the stairs. At the time I had very long ginger hair and a beard, bearing more than a passing resemblance to Catweazle, so I stood there, completely naked, as an inquisitive couple pushed open the door. It was hard to tell who was more terrified. 'It's not a showroom,' I mumbled like a buffoon, and they were gone. Thankfully the showhouse next door was sold fairly soon afterwards and my life is now reasonably normal.

BUTTON PUSHED
Man brings events to a standstill

On what seemed like the hottest day of last summer, while on a particularly tedious and potentially relationship-destroying trip around the local shopping centre with my wife, I found myself stuck on a packed escalator, unable to move due to a large group of coffin-dodgers blocking the route ahead. The escalator seemed to be moving exceptionally slowly and, with sweat running off my head and into my eyes, I suddenly reached the end of my tether. Before I could stop myself, my hand reached out and punched the bright red emergency stop button – a move which brought the moving stairway to an immediate halt. People, including the frail old pensioners, crashed forwards into each other, sending bags and packages flying off in all directions. But amazingly, the crime was never pinned on me. The last thing I remember as I trod over the heap of bodies to escape the carnage was a desperate plea from an innocent little boy, who was being soundly thrashed for 'being so bad'.

HAPPY REUNION
Lover misreads signs

Last year I dumped my girlfriend, explaining that I 'just wasn't ready for what she wanted.' Obviously this caused some upset, and for six months we didn't speak. Then we met, seemingly quite by chance, while out shopping. All went well, and to my surprise she invited me to dinner. I accepted, and we had a fantastic meal, before going on to some bars and a club. That week my boss was on holiday, and as his office was in his house, I had the keys to his pad. We had a great night, but in the morning I awoke to find my ex gone, with a note apologizing for the mess. Staggering downstairs, it was obvious I had been set up. The walls, carpet and most of the stairs were covered in green paint. Furious, I called her house, but she was at work, and when I told her mother what had happened, she actually defended her daughter. I lost it, informed the crazy bitch that it was fairly obvious where my ex got her mental behaviour from, and slammed down the phone. After a futile attempt to scrub off the paint, it was time to call my boss. Terrified, I explained what had happened, but he just laughed. He had knocked the tin of paint down the stairs on his way to the airport, and as he was in a rush he decided to leave it until he got back. The ex called that evening, saying that the only mess she had left was a used coffee cup, her mother was in a state of shock, and she never wanted to see me again.

STRANGE INSTRUCTIONS
Patient stands proud

A few years ago, while working in America, I was struck down with kidney stones and rushed to a plush American hospital for a series of tests. My company was paying the bill, so no expense was spared, and I was appointed my own personal, and attractive, female attendant. I had to lie naked on a table, following instructions such as, 'Tackle to the left please, scrotum to the right,' while my nether-regions were photographed. This was fine until she completely stunned me with the line, 'The doctor would like some of you erect.' She said that she would be back in a few minutes. I then set about raising steam but by the time she came back, the best I had mustered was a lazy lob. She then pointed to another machine standing in the corner. 'I need you to stand up straight for an X-ray,' she said, tears streaming down her face.

FLATMATE REQUIRED
Kindly offer rejected

Just over a year ago I had to find a new flatmate, and ended up scanning the university noticeboard. Among the scruffy notes from homeless students was one from a man named 'Jesus'. I proceeded to phone my list of prospective flatmates, but Jesus wasn't in, so I left a message on his answering machine asking him to come around that evening at nine. I then settled down in front of the TV to wait for the other interviewees to turn up, but nobody came – until, at nine, the doorbell rang. Assuming that Jesus had got the message and decided to come round, I buzzed the guy in and stood at the top of the communal stairwell to greet him. Unlike the kindly, bearded chap I had expected, he was a big, mean-looking man, and I nervously stuck out my hand. 'Hello,' I said. 'Are you Jesus?' He must have stared at me for a full minute before slowly replying, 'No, my name is Heinrich.' Convinced that Jesus was on his way up the stairs and unable to lower my arm through sheer nerves, I looked over his shoulder and said quietly, 'Oh, I was expecting Jesus. Never mind, would you like to come in and see my room?' Without taking his eyes off me, the bloke edged down the stairs, one by one, and left. As I found out next day, the girls living above me were also advertising their flat and Heinrich had been on his way up to view it.

FREUDIAN SLIP
Child stuns family gathering

About ten years ago my mum invited the whole family around for Christmas dinner. After we'd eaten I had the urge to do what most teenage boys do, and disappeared up to my room for a quick spank of the monkey. Mission accomplished, I decided to head out for a sneaky cigarette, but to do that I had to tell my mum I was off out for a walk. I trotted downstairs, entered the packed living room and announced, 'I'm just going for a wank.' To this day my grandad bursts out laughing whenever we all get together.

OLDSTERS TAUNTED
Football fan regrets myopia

While the last World Cup was on, I invited a couple of mates over to watch an England game. Arriving home late – mere minutes before my pals were due to arrive – I raced around to the shop to purchase the necessary beer and crisps, leaving my glasses at home. On the way back I spied the lads cycling up behind me, so – being the crazy guy that I am – I ran away in a comical manner, shouting: 'Oh no! They're gonna get me! Somebody save me!' When I eventually reached my front garden, I held my arms triumphantly aloft and turned around, hollering, 'Come on, you slow fuckers!' – only for the faces of a nice middle-class couple to swim into focus, staring at me as they cycled past. My mates arrived a minute later, by car.

STINKING FISH DRAMA
Angler catches mersey trout

A short while ago I was taking part in a fishing competition on the River Trent. The match money was fairly serious and I was keen not to leave my rod. I was concentrating on a match it looked like I could win and desperately tried to ignore the effects of the previous night's curry and lager as it applied pressure on my bowel. But eventually the call of nature became too much and I had to give in. I trotted off up the bank, found a quiet stretch of river well secluded in high reeds, dropped my all-in-ones and did the business. I then rushed back to my rod and carried on fishing. About half an hour later a heavy downpour started and I pulled up the hood of my all-in-ones. I couldn't believe what I had done. In my earlier haste I had shit into my hood, and ended up with my own turd in my hair and down my back. Even to this day the lads in our fishing club refer to me, with great wit, as Shithead.

CLEAR WINDOWS
Man's privacy invaded

On visiting my mother recently, I discovered that she was having her house altered, placing the bathroom upstairs in what used to be her large front bedroom. There I was, having a morning shit, when the window cleaner arrived and started on the big bathroom window. Now, at this stage of early renovation, the clear glass hadn't been replaced with a frosted version, and so I sat there pretending I couldn't see him for a few minutes, until my bottle went and I ran out into the bedroom with my trousers around my ankles. Once safely behind the wall, I bent down and peeked round the corner so that I could see when he had gone and return to finish the job. And then I heard a noise behind me. Turning around slowly, I found myself looking straight at the cleaner's apprentice doing the other window, staring in wonderment at me bent over, starfish winking, peeking at his boss.

BALLGIRL TAUNTED
Tennis ball fells player

Many years ago my mate Peter asked if I would like to come and play tennis with him at his local club. Neither of us had played much tennis before, so Pete just hit balls at me as hard as he could, which I tried in vain to smash back. Our amateur attempts didn't go unnoticed by the two women on the court next to us, who spent most of the game giggling. And then it happened. One of them started walking towards us to retrieve a ball, just as Pete hammered back a shot. But instead of coming to me, it shot off to the left, straight into the head of the approaching woman, who went down like a sack of shit. There was a stunned silence as we all stared at her in disbelief, broken only by Peter, who was completely oblivious to what he had done, and without looking up, cheerfully shouted, 'Thanks, lady!' as his ball rolled gently to a halt at his feet.

SCORER MIX-UP
Player both on & off pitch

My first assignment as a budding football reporter on my local rag was to cover a game between Sheffield Wednesday and Blackburn. Things started badly before I even got there, when I became mired in traffic about a mile from the ground. I decided to abandon it, and sprinted towards the floodlights. With seconds to spare I barged into the press room, where my dishevelled appearance caused a ripple of laughter from the seasoned reporters and took a seat next to a man from BBC Radio Lancashire and his guest summarizer. Only then did I realize that I had forgotten my team-sheet, but found it easy to guess what was going on, until a sudden goal caused chaos in the press box as everyone disagreed whose foot had put the ball in the back of the net. Sensing a chance to impress my new media colleagues, I cleared my throat and said confidently, 'It was Kevin Gallagher.' There was a murmur of thanks as the journos jotted the name down, and my proud face must have looked a picture when Radio Lancashire's guest summarizer leaned over, nudged me and said, 'I'm Kevin Gallagher.'

SECOND-HAND PURCHASE
Surfer leaves his mark

Not too long ago my boyfriend, who is very tall and of a large build, responded to an advert for a second-hand wet suit. We gave them a call and they told us it was still available, so we went around to have a look. When we got there we were greeted by a couple who seemed deadly keen to sell him a ghastly luminous yellow thing, and although it was clearly too small, my boyfriend politely agreed to try it on. Eventually he returned from the bedroom with the suit pulled up as far as it would go, which was only to his chest. The couple then jumped on him and pulled it right up, giving him a colossal wedgy in the process, and forcing the hood right over his head until he was completely trapped in this horrible suit. Looking hot and red-faced, my boyfriend waddled crab-like back into the bedroom to get changed while I made small talk for what seemed like ages. When he finally returned, however, he had the suit rolled up under his arm, blithely said, '£120 was it, mate?', paid the man, and pulled me out of the house, only to ditch the thing in the first bin we walked past. Apparently when he had pulled the material out from between his bum cheeks, he'd left the world's biggest skid mark on the glowing yellow. He never did go scuba diving.

MARATHON-RUNNER'S MISHAP
Twenty-six stinking miles

It was the morning of the London Marathon. I was ready to run and there were hundreds of us queuing up to use the portaloos at the start. I squeezed into the cubicle, where the floor was awash with runners' pee. While in there, I decided to apply some more Vaseline to my sensitive areas and accidentally dropped my shirt, soaking it in urine. Just then, I heard the PA system announce one minute to the off, looked in horror at my now soaking T-shirt and made the real-men-don't-care-if-their-kit-smells-of-other-peoples'-urine decision. Holding my breath, I pulled my shirt over my head and for the next 26 miles and 385 yards ran as fast as I could. As I worked up a sweat, everyone gave me a wide berth and at the end no-one rushed to congratulate me on finishing in a respectable time.

POTTY TRAINING
Pensioner drowns grandson

A couple of years ago I went for a weekend visit to my parents. My wheelchair-bound gran was due to come round for Sunday lunch and, because the toilet was upstairs, we borrowed a commode from the nursing home next door. The old goat decided she needed to use the thing the minute she got through the door, so I went and waited in the garden until the show was over. However, the pot became stuck to gran's flabby arse and, as mum couldn't shift it by herself, I was summoned to give a hand. Mum pulled gran into a standing position (because she didn't want me to see her lady parts) and with a grim face I squatted down and heaved at the heavy bowl. As if the sight of Nan's flabby white arse wasn't bad enough to put me right off my lunch, when the pot's air-tight seal broke, I toppled over backwards and emptied a near-full tub of hot piss all over myself.

LEAKING BIN TRAUMA
Plumber makes a killing

I returned home to my parents' house after a few beers, absolutely bursting for a pee. Running upstairs to the bathroom, I was surprised to find a decorator doing up the tiling. Not wanting to bother him, I went into my bedroom and in my semi-drunken haze, decided to pee in the metal waste-paper bin and empty it out of the bedroom window later on. After a quick kip, I went downstairs to find my parents looking up at a growing yellowish stain on the wallpaper. My father, thinking it must be a burst pipe had called an emergency plumber. I kept quiet and watched nervously. The plumber arrived and when he'd finished examining the tank in the room next to mine, claimed that it was leaking and some parts needed replacing. The bill came to several hundred pounds. I wanted to tell my folks, but the embarrassment would have been too much.

CHEERY GOODBYE
Soldier grabs wrong body part

While I was doing basic army training at Pirbright, a friend suggested we stay with his aunt and uncle in Reading. They were a most accommodating couple, and we had a delicious meal before returning to camp. When the time came to leave, I shook my friend's uncle by the hand, then bent forward to kiss the aunt on the cheek. As I did so, she appeared to raise her hand, so I went to shake it, and realized straight away that I had got hold of her right tit. I decided to go ahead as if nothing was wrong, and confidently shook her boob. The next week my mate asked if I wanted to go back but I declined – I couldn't face that old dear again.

BODYPART ARRIVES
Man's clothing offends pensioner

Last year, after a crash-course diet, I looked like a beanpole, so I joined the local gym. I decided to wear a loose-fitting Lycra outfit, going on the theory that although it felt baggy now, my impending muscles would soon fill it out. The treadmill was my first port of call, and it wasn't long before I was exchanging pleasantries with a well-built woman next to me. So there I was, jogging away quite happily, when one of her large, firm tits popped straight out of her running-top, giving me the quickest erection of my life. Mercifully she didn't notice, but the old boy on the rowing machine suddenly found himself on eye-level with an exposed penis. He started cursing and waving his fist, and eventually everyone in the gym was aware of my misdemeanour. I was nearly chased out of the place by fuming pensioners, and a week later the gym cancelled my membership. But to be honest, I hadn't planned on going back.

MAN ON GIRL'S BIKE
Road rage hospitalizes cyclist

It seems that whenever my mate and I go out, something terrible happens that makes us chuckle. The other day we were on our way to the pub when a big bloke hammered past us on a really old woman's shopping bike. He looked so stupid on the gimmer's vehicle that the pair of us just burst out laughing, and when he turned to scowl at us he was hit by a passing car. We just stood there pissing ourselves while he picked himself up off the floor, but quickly stopped when he turned to face us with an enraged expression across his purple face. Then he charged at us, and as we were rooted to the spot with fear, he would certainly have caught us, had he not suddenly been mown down by a car going in the opposite direction. I obviously felt truly guilty, as the poor chap was hospitalized, but we still gave him the wanker sign as they loaded him into the ambulance.

HOSPITAL CHAOS
Lazy visitor causes alarm

About two months ago, I found myself in the labour ward with my girlfriend. We had been there for about four hours and as I was by now desperate for a piss, I made my excuses and headed out to find the nearest toilet. When I asked where they were, however, I was told that they were in the adjoining ward, so to save time I dived into a nearby cubicle reserved exclusively for hospital patients. Halfway through relieving myself I had the sudden urge to fart, and I let rip with a trump so smelly that my eyes began to water. It was then that I considered the very real possibility that there could be someone outside waiting to use the toilet after me, and I became rooted to the spot with embarrassment. Reaching up, I gave the extractor chain a tug – but instead of a fan roaring into life, a loud siren went off at the hospital reception, accompanied by a flashing red light giving away my location. It was the emergency cord. Panicking, I pulled again, and the siren became even louder. Suddenly my door was unlocked from the outside and three midwives burst in to find me red-faced, stinking of shit and covering my face in shame. Their laughs were stifled only by the sounds of retching.

CAR-CRIME VICTIM
Pursuer has second thoughts

A few months ago I purchased a bright red MG convertible. I spent an absolute fortune on it, adding extras like a pukka stereo and new wheels, and keeping it in tip-top condition. So you can imagine my fury when, after leaving the top down, I caught a man in the act of dragging his keys down my baby's door! Enraged, I shouted at him, and he shot up the street in terror. I ran after him for miles – we went down alleys, ran through traffic and even jumped over some garden fences. He kept on running, but he couldn't shake me. Finally, I chased him into a dead end. I had the bastard. Or so I thought. Only when he turned, panting, to face me, did I realize that he was a big, mean-looking bastard. He had probably only taken flight out of shock; I, on the other hand, hadn't stopped to think what I would do if I caught him. He took out a car stereo (yep, mine) and approached, smashed me over the head with it and knocked me out. I eventually made it back to my scratched, stereoless car with a huge lump on my head.

POST-MATCH INCIDENT
Tennis fan left hanging

A few summers ago, me and my mates regularly climbed over a spiked steel gate into the school opposite my house to play on their tennis court. One evening I was last man off the premises, which meant lugging home all the tennis gear alone. Laden with bags and racquets, I carefully climbed the gate, swung my legs over, and jumped – catching my shorts on a spike and leaving me swinging six feet in the air. Not only was I suffering from an excruciating wedgie, but the seam in my shorts was cutting into my left testicle. And as if that wasn't embarrassment enough, I could only shout as a pair of young rascals wandered over, poked fun at me then stole all the tennis gear I'd dropped. I was dangling for ten minutes before a friend finally came back and helped me down.

CON UNLOADS
Driver gets face-full

Last Saturday afternoon in Aberdeen, I was sitting in a queue of cars at the traffic lights by the harbour. Parked in front of me was a guy in a white Fiesta van with the window wound down, and alongside him was a cattle truck, with some seriously pissed off cows looking out through the slatted sides. The van driver was propping up his head with his hand, clearly enjoying the summer rays, when suddenly, without any warning, a high-pressure jet of pure bovine piss blasted out of the truck, scoring a direct hit on his head. The bloke tried to get the window up, but it jammed, and he took an entire face-load of warm urine. As the truck moved off, the door burst open and, engaging in a lengthy session of projectile vomiting, the driver stood by his van, steam rising from his body, retching for all he was worth. I shook my head as I passed him, my face a picture of genuine concern, and then, much to his annoyance, I absolutely pissed myself.

TELEPHONE GRIEF
Prankster gets brush-off

A number of years ago, my hospitalized grandfather was rapidly deteriorating in health, and his daughter (my mum) was getting extremely upset. Having received compassionate leave from work, she spent all her free time at his bedside, and most of her nights crying at home. But things took a turn for the worse when she began getting nuisance phone calls. Worried about my mother's state, I agreed to answer the phone. Each time the thing rang, there was no answer, just silence. Getting more and more annoyed with the situation, I picked up the next call and yelled a stream of abuse at the sod on the other end, then slammed the phone down. The calls ceased. The next day, however, my grandfather's nurse phoned to say that the old man was upset that he couldn't get in contact with us, and would we please call him. It was then, while speaking to gramps, that the situation hit home. The 'crank' was grandad, and he hadn't realized that he had to press 'Answer' on the payphone when his call was picked up. Not only that, but he'd heard me clear as a bell when I'd asked if he wanted to smell my stinking underwear.

FISHING FIASCO
Man gets lucky bite

The morning after a night on the bevy, my friend's grandfather and his mates decided to go out fishing on Loch Lomond. The group set off in a small boat, but as the choppy water combined with the effects of the previous night's drinking, the grandfather puked his load over the side. His retching was so violent that it dislodged his false teeth and the men watched helplessly as they sunk into the depths of the Loch.

He was livid, but his friends refused to interrupt their fishing trip, and by the time they'd had their lunch he'd calmed down enough to enjoy a short nap. On seeing this, one of the friends took out his false teeth and tied them to a fishing line. When the grandfather awoke, his friend shouted, 'I've got a bite!' and began reeling in his line. To the grandfather's delight, the false teeth were on the end. 'Would you credit it,' he said. 'That must be a one in a million chance.' Giving them a quick clean, he popped the teeth into his mouth. But he gave a puzzled look when he discovered they didn't fit. His friends were in knots of laughter, until he took out the teeth, said, 'They're not mine,' and flung them back into the Loch.

SMELL OF FEAR

Lodger taken for a pervert

A friend of mine moved into a house, sharing it with his 40-something, spinster landlady. He was the ideal lodger, and always ready to help with the dishes. One day he woke up late for work and, trying to do three things at once, put the toast on and went upstairs. When he returned to the kitchen, he found to his horror that it was full of smoke. The toast had turned to carbon. Opening windows, he prayed that the landlady wouldn't discover his mistake. Eventually the fumes cleared and he was just about to leave when he spotted a laden clothes horse in the corner. Afraid that it would reek of smoke, he lifted an item of clothing and sniffed. It was fine. At the same moment, his landlady appeared in her dressing gown and gasped in horror. He looked at her, she looked at him, he looked down to see that he'd been sniffing a rather stained pair of old frillies.

SPOOKY PRANK
Grown man scared out of house

A few years ago, I was staying overnight at a friend's house with a group
of mates, when we got talking about the paranormal. One of our group,
Mike, consistently told us to stop taking the piss, as 'playing with the
Devil' was no laughing matter. Naturally, this just made the rest of us tell
stories of a more and more extreme nature. Eventually Mike got so pissed
off and upset that he went to bed. The rest of us stayed up talking for a
while, then decided to round off the night with a little practical joke. We
waited until we thought Mike would be asleep, then snuck downstairs
and began scratching at his door, expecting him to tell us to piss off and
go to bed. Instead, we heard an almighty smash followed by a loud
scream. We opened the bedroom door to see that Mike had hurled a chair
through the window and jumped through, slashing his legs severely as he
did so. We no longer mess with the Dark Side.

FOOTBALL TERRACE SHOCK
Man was blinded by pie

I was at a recent Liverpool match where Michael Owen was about to
stroll in a hat-trick. As I rose to acknowledge my hero, my world went
brown. Screaming in agony, it felt like I'd gone blind in my right eye, and
my forehead and ear seemed alight. My first reaction was that I had a
brain tumour which had exploded in the excitement. My worst fears
appeared to be confirmed as I examined the brown and white matter
emanating from my head. As the goal euphoria dissipated, a number
of my fellow supporters began to laugh at my hideous condition. 'It's
pie lad, pie in yer eye!'

An over-enthusiastic fan to my rear had, at the moment of scoring,
ejaculated his lunch up in the air with myself as unlucky recipient. Apart
from a pleasant lady from St Helens who provided tissues, the Tarbys of
the crowd set about belittling my injuries with talk of dieting and steak
and kidney in the sky. Bastards!

PRE-MED APPLIED
Confused patient dresses up

Last July I found myself in hospital for an operation to straighten my nose. After my pre-med injection, the nurse gave me a green robe and small hat, and left me to get changed. Pulling the curtain around the bed to avoid prying eyes, I was horrified to find that the dressing gown didn't fit, and as the strings were far too short, I had a choice: I could leave the front half of my body exposed, or my arse. I opted for the latter, pulled back the curtains and gently sat on the bed. By now I was starting to feel the effects of the injection, so I put on the hat, and waited for the nurse. I noticed that the man in the bed opposite was staring. Not only that, but everyone in the ward was looking at me, and a nurse walked past, desperately trying not to laugh. Clearly, the joke was on me, but in my confused state I couldn't work out why. Defeated, I scratched my head, only to be surprised that, despite my hat, I could still feel my hair. Further exploration revealed that the garment had two large holes, but before I could do any more, a near hysterical nurse took me into the operating theatre and stuck another needle in me. As I realized what had happened, I gently passed out in the knowledge that there was a pair of pants on my head.

SEEDY STARGAZER
Astronomer wrongly accused

When the Hale-Bop comet was in our skies I spent a lot of my evenings looking at it with my binoculars from my back garden. It was a good place to view because it was dark and nobody could see me. More recently, I heard about the dramas occurring on the Mir space station, which I also heard was visible at night, moving from east to west. One night I thought I would try to see it, and I went into my garden, which faces east, and began to look. It started to cloud over, and without thinking I went to the front of the house and continued to peer through my binoculars. I couldn't see anything, but when I dropped my binoculars from my eyes I noticed that my next-door-neighbours were looking over at me. They thought I had been trying to catch one of them stripping off in the bedroom window, and called me a pervert. To this day I have never had a chance to explain what I was doing, so they probably still think I am some kind of Peeping Tom.

MAN DOWN
Trauma amuses shopper

A few years ago, my girlfriend and I decided to visit a shopping centre on the outskirts of town. It's the type of establishment that claims to provide a great day out for all the family, with cafés, rides, displays and a couple of people in bear costumes. When we got there I followed my girlfriend into the store, and paused to watch two ladies give a First Aid demonstration in a cordoned-off section, which had previously held a display of vintage motorcycles. As the pair rolled the dummy onto its back, however, part of its internal mechanism popped out through its trousers, giving the impression that it had a huge wooden hard-on. Naturally I thought this was brilliant, and I shouted to my girlfriend to come and see the awesome spectacle, but she just ignored me and walked away. Puzzled by her lack of interest, I turned back to the demonstration, only to find that both women were staring at me, clearly furious. It was then that I realized that the 'dummy' was actually an unfortunate lad in his early twenties, suffering from a fit and being resuscitated by two passing shoppers.

CULTURE SHOCK
Thief gets just desserts

About two years ago, while I was living with four friends, I contracted a particularly vicious strain of thrush. The doctor gave me a prescription, but it was proving useless against the fungal onslaught. A friend had told me that natural yogurt was the answer, so off to the supermarket I went, and bought the biggest pot they had. Back home, I placed the afflicted bodypart into the pot and soaked it for an hour or so. Bliss! I put the yogurt in the fridge so that I could treat myself again later – but when I returned to repeat the treatment, the pot had vanished. I was horrified. Who had stolen my yogurt? Eventually one of my flatmates confessed. I never had the balls to tell him where the yogurt had been before he had eaten it, but served him right, thieving bastard! I'm sure he had very bad breath and an unusually aggressive case of plaque over the next week.

BRUSHES WITH
THE LAW

HE WAS FRAMED, GUV
Look-alike is shopped

When *Crimewatch* was at its peak some years ago, my friends and I
always wished we knew the criminals featured. Until one day when we
recognized one of our workmates – or at least someone uncannily like
him. Now, we all knew that at the time of the 'transvestite flashing' our
workmate was with us. He was an innocent man. But did that stop us?
Did it fuck! It just had to be done. Just for a laugh, you understand, I
phoned the police ... The ensuing scene was like something out of *The Bill*.
A police van, loaded with coppers, pulled up outside. They burst in,
grabbed our poor unsuspecting colleague, and bundled him into the van.
The next day, the CID questioned us; had we noticed anything 'suspicious'
about our colleague's recent behaviour? Was he a 'washing line thief'?
Needless to say, we were too scared to tell the police the truth; someone
claimed to have caught him reading a copy of *Golden Shower* in the toilets.
Fortunately our mate was let off through a lack of evidence. He was last
heard of living in a hostel in Oldham, after his wife left him.

KIDNAP DISASTER
Just having a laugh, officer

Myself, my brother and a fairly strange mate decided to kidnap another
pal's three younger brothers whom he babysits on Wednesdays. The plan
went like this: having assembled a pick-axe handle, a metal pipe and a
length of chain, we'd enter the house with woolly hats over our faces
and tie our mate up while one of us ran around shouting, 'Where's the
fucking kids?' We'd then leave empty-handed, get changed in the car and
go back in to 'rescue' our mate – thus, he'd be eternally in our debt. So,

the door opens and we rush in. My brother runs upstairs shouting, 'Where's the fucking kids?' while we grab our mate, Simon, who puts up a fight. A very bad move, as Peter, the strange mate, seems to revel in inflicting pain and starts punching Simon. It all goes horribly wrong. Simon develops breathing problems, so my brother and I take our masks off and tell him it's only a joke. But our apologies are cut short as the house is stormed by police. Unbeknown to us, Simon had been on the blower to his girlfriend and, still on the phone while he answered the door, she'd heard the shouting and called the police. We tried to explain to the coppers why three grown men got their larks by virtually giving another of their mates a heart attack. His girlfriend didn't find it funny either.

ILLEGAL BOOZE
Helping hand is crushed

A couple of weeks ago I was walking through Leicester after a night at the pictures when, on the way to the bus station, I was approached by two young girls who wanted me to go to the off licence to buy some alcopops for them. For no good reason, I agreed, and they gave me a fiver. But once inside the offie, the man behind the till asked me if the girls outside were with me, and when I said yes, he refused to serve me. I went out and told the girls this, and they insisted I try the offie across the road. So I went into the second offie, picked up the bottles and went to pay the woman behind the counter, who had some trouble with the till. And by the time I came to pay, the door flew open and two coppers came in and nicked me for buying booze for minors. I was then dragged to the station, kept for three hours and released with a warning. On my release, the two girls were outside the nick, with a big bloke who came over and twatted me for nicking a fiver from his sister.

TASTELESS PRANK
Mates terrorize takeaway

After an all-day drinking session, my mate and I came across a dead cat spread-eagled in the road. My mate, ever the prankster, picked it up and, to my horror, calmly walked into the local Chinese takeaway, threw the recently deceased moggy on the counter and announced, 'Right, that's the LAST you're getting! Until you pay for the last dozen, NO MORE CATS!' Then he left. Five seconds later, the restaurant was emptied of its horrified customers, and the irate takeaway owner was hurling abuse at us. We decided that a tactical withdrawal was necessary, and legged it. After a quarter of a mile, we calmed ourselves down by popping into the offie for a six-pack. Quenching our thirst, we were surprised by the police, complete with the irate owner claiming, 'Those are the bastards who scared off my customers!' We were consequently bunged in the back of the van, interrogated and charged with various offences, from breaching the peace to cruelty to animals – all of which I pleaded not guilty to, especially cruelty to animals, which I argued was somewhat difficult as the creature was already dead. Unimpressed, they chucked us into separate cells until 6 am the next day. The case eventually got to court, raising a few laughs from the public gallery. I got a ticking off, but my mate's £250 payout to the takeaway owner for loss of takings meant that we're right off Chinese at the moment.

WORRYING FOOTBALL STORY
Copper loses rag

On one of my rare trips from North Wales up to Turf Moor, the home of Burnley FC, I had the usual hassles of Saturday afternoon parking near the ground. After a frustrating 20 minutes dashing round nearby housing estates I eventually spotted a place about 100 yards up the road. On approaching the spot, a police squad car passed me from the opposite direction and I noticed the uniformed driver waving his half-clenched fist at me in a long masturbatory gesture. I flashed him a 'V' sign thinking him prejudiced against Burnley fans – I was wearing my claret and blue home shirt. There was a screech of brakes and the car reversed. An angry policeman got out. 'What do you think you're playing at, mate?' he said. 'Well, you called me a wanker,' I replied, sheepishly. 'Actually, sir,' he said, 'I was telling you to put your seatbelt on.'

CAR LOVERS
Mini lust is curtailed

On a night out with my girlfriend, the only place where we could truly be alone together was in my car, a Mini 1000, which we parked in a deserted lane before getting down to business. As I am 6 ft 2 in, there was a lack of space and so we continued up against the side of the car. Suddenly we were startled by the glare of oncoming headlights. My date had the presence of mind to dive into the passenger door, but I remained in the road, transfixed like a rabbit. Eventually, I came to my senses and ran to get in the driver's side. But I discovered the door had been locked – not by me, but by my (soon to be ex) girlfriend, who was finding the escapade very amusing. Acting on instinct, I went to the front of the car, lifted the bonnet and pretended to be the victim of a breakdown. What I didn't reckon on was the car being driven by two members of the local constabulary, who had decided to help me out – only to find me with one shoe on, my trousers held up by one hand and my shirt tucked into my boxers. What gave the game away was the huge erection bulging in my pants. I tried to maintain a front by saying it must be a dodgy ignition circuit. 'Can't see what's so exciting about a few spark plugs, sir!' said one policeman as they burst into laughter, looking at the large bulge in my pants.

BREAKING THE LAW
Boozer takes the wheel

I have only broken the law once in my life and, sadly, crime paid. I had put in for my driving test and was given a date for the nerve-racking day. Unfortunately, the date the DVLC had given me was one day after my 18th birthday. I worked out that I would have to stop my birthday boozing at around 9 pm in order to be clear for the test the following morning. So, on my birthday I went out, promising my girlfriend on pain of death that I would stick to two or three pints, and be tucked up in bed by ten o'clock. Needless to say, I got shit-faced. Furthermore, I stayed out until 6.30 in the morning, deciding that I would cancel my test due to illness. The following morning, when I'd had only three hours' sleep, my girlfriend came round, unannounced, and dragged me out of bed to get me ready for the test. I didn't have the nerve to tell her I had been on the piss all night, so, fuelled with tea and a packet of mints, I went down to the test centre. Maybe it was the booze, or maybe I'm just a great driver, but anyway, I passed. I'm possibly the only man who qualified to drive while under the influence. And I'm ashamed of myself.

CAR CALAMITY
With friends like this ...

On the night of my graduation ball, my mate left his keys and car at my house so we wouldn't do anything foolish. As we were drinking ourselves under the table, I came across a girl I had lusted after for several terms, and I charmed the wench in no time. Soon, on a short stumble back to my place, we started craving a pizza. I suggested that she drive my friend's car to a take-away. We'd hardly got in before we were going at it hammer and tongs. Halfway through, we were shocked to hear, 'What the fuck is going on?' It was my mate – he'd brought his spare key to the ball and had headed back to his car for a kip. Within seconds, he'd fallen into an alcoholic slumber, so the lovely lady and I continued as before. Then, fully sated, we set off – but women's driving being what it is, she took a bend too sharply and ended up on the other side of the road up a bank. Suddenly sober, I got out of the car, and dragged my groaning friend into the driver's seat. I told my lady friend to go back to the flat while I moved into the passenger seat, pouring whisky over myself, and waited for a passer-by. Soon the Old Bill were with us. I tried playing the 'pissed-as-a-fart passenger' as me and my still-oblivious pal were dragged off to the local cop shop. He remembers nothing of the night, other than what I told him: that he'd insisted on going to get a pizza. He lost his licence for two years; I got a night in the cells. I have since married that appalling driver – and when I told my one-time friend the truth some years later it earned me a broken nose and six stitches. Still, that was a bloody good piss-up.

SPEAKER LEFT ON
Learner receives blue criticism

Some years ago I was working for a small business firm in Manchester. On the way home I was just about to drive up onto the M26, when I had to stop at a red light. In front of me was a police car, a Jaguar, then a learner. When the lights turned green the learner started to pull away, stalled, and couldn't restart his car until the lights were red again. When they changed to green, he stalled again, prompting the man in the Jag to get out and walk towards him. Suddenly the police car loudspeaker burst into life: 'Would the gentleman who has just left his vehicle please remember he was once a learner too.' Clearly embarrassed, the man returned to his Jag. As the lights changed, the learner stalled again, when we were treated to, 'Fucking hell, the dozy twat has done it again.'

COUPLE ON THE RUN
Girlfriend rattled by crash

A while back, my uncle wanted to impress his girlfriend with a day out in the country, so he borrowed my dad's car – despite not being insured to drive it. He set off with his girlfriend ... and not long into the journey dinged another car. Having no insurance details to swap he sped away from the scene of the accident, hiding the car in a field while the police cruised around, trying to find him. He managed to avoid the rozzers before finally ringing his sister to ask her to come and pick them up from the middle of the countryside. On the way home they stuck to the back roads, and his sister, enjoying all the odours nature has to offer, declared: 'Wow, you can really smell that fresh country air.' 'No,' my uncle had to tell her, 'I'm afraid that's my girlfriend.' She had literally shit herself from fear of being caught by the law.

STUPID BOYS
Aquatic prank turns nasty

A few years ago, during a particularly hot summer, some friends and I visited a local toy store and bought a load of super-powerful water pistols. After several hours of shooting at each other, we got a bit bored and decided to hit the streets in search of new victims. We jumped into my mate's car and began to squirt innocent pedestrians, making good our escape at high speed. Eventually we got bored of this too, and were just about to head for home when we saw a man laden down with shopping bags. We knew that we had to whack him. We slowed to a crawl for the drive-by, lowered the windows, and treated the man to a full-on, four-rifle assault. The poor sod was saturated, and as we sped away we looked back and laughed at him standing soaked and bewildered with his shopping spread out all over the pavement. Later that evening, we were all heading for a night out on the town when we noticed the blue flashing light of the Old Bill in our rear-view mirror. We were rather bemused by this as we hadn't been drinking, and we certainly hadn't been speeding, so we pulled over to the side of the road confident we were safe. The policeman walked up to us, tapped on the window and said, with a smile, 'Alright boys, where's the water pistols?' It was the bloke we had drenched. He then ticketed us for speeding, and made sure we knew he would be keeping a special eye open for our car in the future.

UNLIKELY AUTO OCCURRENCE
Drunken roundabout prang

After a very drunken evening at a party, a friend of mine foolishly decided to drive home. After about a mile, he started going round a roundabout, but realized he'd missed his exit. He stopped the car and started reversing. Then, to his horror, a car went into the back of him. His immediate thought was: 'I'm doomed', especially as he's a lorry driver and would almost definitely lose his licence. Things then went from bad to worse as a police car arrived on the scene. My friend watched the policeman talk to the driver in the rear car. His heart dropped when the policemen walked over to his car and motioned for my friend to lower his window. Putting on his most sober voice, my friend said: 'Evening, officer.' 'It's all right, sir,' the policeman replied, 'you can go. That driver must be completely plastered – he said you were reversing round the roundabout!'